I truly believe that my friend Kyle Winkler has written a profound and poignant book to awaken a generation to the schemes, lies, and deceptions of the enemy! In *Silence Satan* every reader is called to take a journey from failure to freedom and authority. Every Christian must come to crossroads of choosing, to go to the noose or to the nails, to be hung or to be held. Get ready to experience the power of living louder than Satan's voice and stronger than his lies! God has called you to win! Kyle speaks from the heart of a man who has experienced the amazing love of God and His redemptive power! This book is destined to be a classic!

—PATRICK SCHATZLINE
Evangelist and president of Mercy Seat Ministries
Author of *Why Is God So Mad at Me?* and *I Am Remnant*

Through the candid sharing of his own experiences and an extensive study in God's Word, Kyle leads readers on a journey to the foot of the cross where they are reminded of their identity and standing in Christ. *Silence Satan* is a must-read for all believers, but particularly those struggling to overcome the lies of the enemy. I believe this book will draw you closer to Christ, and He will use it to help you be more effective for your unique calling in the kingdom.

—TODD MULLINS
Lead pastor of Christ Fellowship
Palm Beach Gardens, FL

Kyle Winkler's book, *Silence Satan*, is a new twist on "how-to" books! Kyle gives wonderful insight into the realm of spiritual warfare, but with powerful viewpoints of victory through Christ. The personal testimony is compelling, and I know

everyone who reads Winkler's book will be launched ahead in their spiritual pilgrimages!

—Dr. Evon G. Horton
Senior pastor of Brownsville Assembly
Pensacola, FL

I was privileged to first meet Kyle Winkler during an interview he did with evangelist Steve Hill. This was one of Steve's last before passing on to glory. It became apparent within minutes that Kyle is a fellow soldier and a man who burns with a genuine passion to see people have an encounter with God. That broadcast became a mini revival meeting and has now impacted thousands around the world.

Now with his ear turned to heaven, Kyle has put pen to paper and laid out a battle plan that should embolden every believer. *Silence Satan* is a message that is centered upon the cross and will enable you to take hold of the abundant life Christ promised while laying waste to the works of the enemy.

—Daniel K. Norris
Evangelist for Steve Hill Ministries

Kyle Winkler is a man with a profound passion to see people transformed by God's power. This passion oozes from every page. His experience with spiritual warfare is sure to touch many men and women of all ages, because his story is their stories. At a time when we're tempted to find our solutions upon the latest religious bandwagon, it's refreshing to be reminded that the solution was there all along at the cross. *Silence Satan* delivers upon its promise and is sure to give you the boost you need to get up and get on with fulfilling God's mission for your life.

—Buford Lipscomb
President of Liberty Network International

At last—a book that clearly discloses the greatest weapon for overcoming Satan's influence in our lives. Today the body of Christ has many helpful methods of deliverance, but Kyle Winkler has captured the pinnacle of truth in his book *Silence Satan*. By humbly and vulnerably telling his own story of how he grappled with the enemy, Winkler then relates how he found victory at the precise place where Satan was defeated—at the foot of the cross. He shows how the cross is the "ultimate gotcha," for indeed the instrument on which Satan meant to defeat Jesus is the very instrument that defeated Satan. Kyle then explains how we can use that same lethal weapon to defeat the enemy in our own lives.

This book will kindle in your heart a fresh love for the cross of Jesus as you are challenged to look up and "behold the Lamb." Winkler calls the church back to the cross where we can focus on Jesus until every enemy falls at the bleeding feet of the Lamb. Not only does Winkler call you to gaze more deeply at the crucified and risen Christ, but he also shows you how to apply the authority of the cross and the power of Christ's blood to every situation in your life. I recommend this book to all who long to live every day in victory through the power of the shed blood of Jesus Christ.

—SANDY DAVIS KIRK, PHD
Author and president of America Ablaze Ministries

SILENCE SATAN

KYLE WINKLER

CHARISMA
HOUSE

Most CHARISMA HOUSE BOOK GROUP products are available at special quantity discounts for bulk purchase for sales promotions, premiums, fund-raising, and educational needs. For details, write Charisma House Book Group, 600 Rinehart Road, Lake Mary, Florida 32746, or telephone (407) 333-0600.

SILENCE SATAN by Kyle Winkler
Published by Charisma House
Charisma Media/Charisma House Book Group
600 Rinehart Road
Lake Mary, Florida 32746
www.charismahouse.com

Cover design by Lisa Rae Cox
Design Director: Justin Evans

Visit the author's website at www.kylewinkler.org.

Library of Congress Control Number: 2014939997
International Standard Book Number: 978-1-62136-655-3
E-book ISBN: 978-1-62136-656-0

15 16 17 18 19 — 9 8 7 6 5 4 3 2
Printed in the United States of America

To those who tread beyond a comfort
zone on an audacious pursuit of God

CONTENTS

Introduction: My Story. 1

SECTION I: A BATTLE RAGES

1 You've Been Set Up. 9

2 The Profile of the Accuser 21

3 The Devil's Playbook 35

SECTION II: THE PLACE OF VICTORY

4 The Noose or the Nails. 49

5 Behold the Lamb. 61

6 The Blood That Speaks 75

7 Marching 'em Naked. 89

8 No Loitering! 103

SECTION III: LIVING IN VICTORY

9 The Place of God's Delight. 121

10 The Uniform of the Righteous 137

11 Shut Up, Devil! 153

12 The Voice of Truth 167

13 Speak Up! 185

Appendix: More Satan-Silencing Scriptures
to Speak Aloud 197

Notes. 201

Acknowledgments 205

About the Author. 207

Introduction

MY STORY

WITHOUT WARNING A SUBTLE BUT NAGGING voice perched upon my shoulder and whispered, "Look what you've done!" This redirected my mind's eye to just about every regretful moment, all the way back to potty training.

Suddenly I saw myself at five years old, shoplifting a piece of chocolate taffy from the grocery store candy bin...then, slightly older, taking a Louisville Slugger to the neighbor girl's stomach, knocking the wind out of her for no good reason (as if there's ever a good reason to do something like that!). I flashed back to the church service when I psyched out the usher, making the man believe that my clenched fist had money for the offering, when instead all I dropped in was a wad of nothing.

Though in these several instances the sounds of dad's belt clearing belt loops paid my penance, there was no infraction too small or too distant for the devil to bring back to my remembrance.

So much more condemning, however, were the poignant reminders of the secret sins of my adult life—of course, the jealousy, unforgiveness, and occasional temper; but especially all the lust I had allowed into my eyes, ears, and mind. Visions of shameful desires and the places those had led all bounced back and forth through my memory like dirty laundry in a never-ending "tumble" cycle.

Throughout the years my most heinous sins had to remain under wraps or be spoken of only in generalities, so that the "I've-got-it-all-together" façade of a budding preacher wouldn't be tarnished. Truthfully, though, I saw myself too often held captive to the flesh and its whims. So when the devil launched the second fiery whisper, "God can't use you!", I began to believe it myself.

"You're a hypocrite!" replayed through my mind. My passion ever since I was sixteen years old was and is to encourage people toward a deep relationship with God. I revel to share about the transformational power of God that I've personally witnessed break addictions and disease. Still, I questioned, "How can I talk about these things and urge others into a Spirit-filled life if I'm not living it perfectly myself?"

By now the moment was ripe for Satan to uncover the final page of his playbook: "Shut it all down!" The ministry. The website. The social network posts. The ambitions to preach to the world. "Walk away. Hang it up. You're too far gone. You've messed up one too many times. You can't live a life worthy of God's service, much less of the miracle-working power you pray to flow through you."

Throughout the following week my mind was the battlefield in a severe demonic war intended to shut me up. Those three assaults—"Look what you've done! God can't use you! Shut it all down!"—plagued me and, on more than one occasion, beat me to tears.

My Story Is Your Story

I've met too many people with similar stories to mine. Perhaps it's surprising to you (or not!), but many are fellows in ministry. They are youth leaders, small group facilitators, worship leaders, or senior pastors, secretly held captive by sin and shame. They greatly desire godliness and want to serve God in powerful ways, yet they can't seem to break the sin cycle. Like the apostle Paul, they confess they continually fall to the very things they hate (Rom. 7:15), and the devil never fails to arrive with nagging reminders of their failures.

Others are victims of the sins of yesterday; their pasts are checkered with unspeakable things, and guilt and shame convince them they'll never be good enough for God.

The stories of many people contain a little of both.

Perhaps you too can relate. Maybe even now there's a voice whispering in your ear, "Put the book down. Don't waste your time. God's moved on to someone less messed up. He can't use you."

The Key to Victory

As I'll unfold throughout this book, in the midst of my spiritual warfare God showed me the key to ending this all. It wasn't another song, souped-up sermon, or resource. Some newfangled religious gimmick wasn't going to do it anymore. No, I had to go back to the basics. It was time for me to face the crux of Christianity—the old, rugged cross.

I must admit, when God revealed to me that the cross was the answer, I was a little let down. I'd known about the cross for years, I thought. Jesus suffered, died, and rose again. This is Christianity 101. What more is there to know? "Give me something deeper," I begged. I wanted a vision in the Spirit of some sensational strategy that no one had ever heard.

But throughout my week of intense battle I realized that while I *knew about* the cross, I didn't truly *know* the cross. So the Holy Spirit led me there, on an intimate journey to the foot of Calvary, where I beheld Jesus in His place of victory as I never had before. In this moment I felt firsthand what Paul meant when he boasted that our record of wrongs was nailed to the cross. I vividly experienced why he said that it's at Calvary where Satan is ultimately dethroned and silenced in our lives.

> ...erasing the record that stood against us with its legal demands. He set this aside, nailing it to the cross. He disarmed the rulers and authorities and made a public example of them, triumphing over them in it.
> —COLOSSIANS 2:14–15

I didn't need some super-spiritual, new strategy. *The cross is the strategy!* God showed me that the cross was His plan established all along to rescue you and me from sin and shame and give us a life of victory. It should never become too familiar. In fact, every answer and solution to the situations we face are found there—not new—but always fresh.

When I finally encountered the cross in its entire splendor, its nails unleashed me. Since that day I've never felt so much freedom. I've never had so much boldness. I arose from my weeping and shaking as one no longer influenced by the voice of Satan, but with a resurrected voice of my own—determined to tell my story.

Let's Go

Framed around my story, this book will lead you to the same place the Lord led me. We'll journey together down that road to Calvary to behold Jesus in His place of victory. I promise it will be unlike any encounter you've had before. Then you'll discover how to live in this place, where the things that the devil meant for your defeat actually defeat him instead.

Come along. Join me on this journey to finally silence Satan and *live* victoriously.

Section I

A BATTLE RAGES

Chapter 1

YOU'VE BEEN SET UP

OU AND I LIVE AT AN UNPARALLELED TIME IN history. Technological advances afford us opportunities that other generations couldn't fathom. Think about some of the innovations within just the last one hundred years. In 1959 the world saw the introduction of something called the microchip. This paved way for the rise of the videocassette recorder (VCR) in the sixties and seventies, which for the first time allowed us to capture events and replay them over and over again. The seventies also birthed the personal computer—arguably the most significant invention with the greatest impact in the history of the world.

Within just a couple decades a worldwide network of these personal computers was popularized to bring something we can no longer imagine life without—the Internet. It wasn't long before phones and devices of all sorts were connected to this digital superhighway, so today we have instant access to virtually anything from anywhere. Technology snowballs so quickly these days that it's hard to imagine what even tomorrow might bring. Who knows what revolutionary gizmo or gadget will be released by the time you read this book.

Jesus spoke about a day in the future when the gospel would be proclaimed throughout the world (Matt. 24:14). In fact, this was the mission with which He tasked the church. "Go into all the world and proclaim the good news to the whole creation," He charged (Mark 16:15). "Be my witnesses...to the ends of the earth" (Acts 1:8). For more than two thousand years now Christians have passionately worked to accomplish this Great Commission, believing, as Jesus assured, that He will return in glory when all people have heard this good news (Matt. 24:14).

I believe the age of which Jesus foretold is here. The days that the church dreamed to see are upon us. Our newfangled technology allows us to take our voices to the corners of the earth without ever leaving our couches. A simple YouTube video made in an apartment in America today can change a life in the slums of India tomorrow. A 140-character tweet can instantly inject a shot of truth and encouragement into someone you never knew existed. Reaching the world no longer takes much money or great ability. In fact, it doesn't take much more than savviness. The possibility of you and I witnessing the realization of the Great Commission is greater than ever before.

A World-Changing Generation

The effects of all of this connectedness upon today's generation are fascinating. It's made our worlds smaller and our voices bigger. It's reshaped our thinking, behaviors, and especially the expectations we have for our lives. Even our fears are different. We're not as concerned with the things that those before us dreaded. For example, it's been famously reported that the greatest fear of those in previous decades was public speaking. Even before death, loneliness, or finances, people grew dizzy at the idea of addressing a crowd.[1]

But the times have certainly changed. In our media-driven,

always-connected world, people are no longer as apprehensive about being in front of others. In fact, many actually seek out opportunities to get their voices heard above the crowds.

Still, if it's not public speaking, death, or finances, what is most concerning to those of us today? A big salary? A fancy car? A spouse? Nada. Perhaps it shouldn't be much of a surprise. *The greatest fear of people today is living a life that doesn't make a difference.*[2]

Think about that. Isn't it one of your greatest desires to make a difference in this world? I know it is mine. Perhaps nothing motivates me more than the opportunity to have an impact. I've moved a thousand miles, taken pay cuts, and teetered along the edge of the risk of failure all for the chance to change lives. And so have many of you.

Today's generation passionately leads church groups, community organizations, and campaigns for charities that we believe in. We long to be world changers and life givers. We equate success with significance. More than the generations before us, we believe we were each brought into this life for a radical mission. We aren't pew warmers or back-of-the-church sitters. No, you and I desperately want to be used by God. And we're often intensely frustrated until we discover what we believe is His purpose for our existence.

Today is a monumental moment in Christianity. Not only do we have the abilities through technology and media to reach the world, but we also have the hunger. I believe we are on the verge of a perfect storm that could accomplish the Great Commission, spread Christ's glory throughout the earth, and usher in His magnificent return. And the devil is scared stiff.

Satan's Foresight

While Satan isn't all knowing, I believe he can sense things in the spirit realm before they happen in the natural. If he perceives something ahead that's detrimental to his cause, he'll bring about resistance in an effort to prevent it. Heightened seasons of spiritual warfare should be our first heads-up that God has something remarkable in store.

Just before I made my first major step into ministry, I began to suddenly deal with things that I never knew existed within me. For months I grew strangely restless and felt as if my faith was running on empty. Out of nowhere my passion waned, and I struggled to pray and worship with as much fervency as I once did. Nobody could understand what was happening within me. And so I began to isolate myself from friends, which only caused more conflict and grief. It seemed as if my emotions were all amplified ten times what they normally were. Even temptations that were never before issues for me suddenly became major issues.

At the time I couldn't pinpoint what started this several-month funk. But eventually it all became very clear. I had been praying so long for God to use me in greater ways of ministry. I knew since high school that He had a call upon my life for something other than what I was doing at the time. And now, just out of college, I was anxious to step into it.

Still, I didn't know just how soon God would answer my prayers. But obviously Satan did. A few months into this warfare an opportunity for a full-time ministry position was offered to me. With shaking legs, butterflies in my stomach, and almost no support from friends and family I took the offer. Not surprisingly, upon assuming the position, all the increased emotions, temptations, and warfare instantly ceased. When Satan realized that he had lost the battle to hold me back, he moved on.

Now, many years later, I reflect upon the opportunity I accepted as the season that prepared me most for the ministry I lead today. I certainly understand why the devil fought so hard in the days leading up to my move. Had he succeeded in obstructing me, I may not be writing this book today.

What I experienced is actually a fairly common strategy of the devil that we notice throughout Scripture, especially approaching times of great spiritual victory. When God was about to deliver the nation of Israel out of their slavery from Egypt, Satan launched a vicious culture war. God had planned to raise up a leader in order to deliver His people into freedom. But the devil was determined to do everything within his power to stop it.

Satan influenced Egypt's pharaoh to be concerned about the strength and power of the Hebrew people. And in fear that these people might eventually overthrow his rule, he ordered every newborn male to be thrown into the Nile River (Exod. 1:22). Moses, the man God chose to lead His people, was born during these days. But despite Satan's greatest efforts, God's plan prevailed—and Moses eventually became the deliverer who led the Israelites out of their bondage.

Of course, the Exodus story foreshadows the days of Christ, through whom God would provide the ultimate deliverance of His people. Here again Satan attempted his same strategy. Hearing of the birth of Jesus, King Herod felt threatened and ordered all children two years or younger to be killed (Matt. 2:16). But even with this all-out assault on the culture, the devil couldn't circumvent God's plan.

Satan's Setup

The apostle Paul referred to Satan's tactics as "his designs" (2 Cor. 2:11). In other words, his strategies are a unique set of blueprints, schemes, and plays intended to produce a certain result. Jesus warned us what Satan's intended result is.

The thief comes only to steal and kill and destroy.
—JOHN 10:10

Satan's purpose is destruction—every time. The devil arrives on the scene like a smart bomb, zeroed in on a specific target for nothing other than absolute demolition. And we should know that as members of a generation with so much potential, you and I are especially within the crosshairs of his scope.

Satan perceives that through us God is up to something on a grand scale. As we draw closer to the fulfillment of the Great Commission, he fears that his days are numbered, and he must pull out all the stops to try to thwart the fulfillment. So like in the days of Moses and Jesus, the devil has upped the ante and again launched a vigorous assault upon the culture.

After the intense spiritual battle that I described in the Introduction, the Lord showed me in detail three secrets of Satan's culture warfare strategy. He revealed that long before you and I were born, Satan devised a series of progressive events intended to destroy our generation before we even have a chance. "It's a setup," God said. And He instructed me, in the same way Paul instructed, to expose this design "so that we may not be outwitted by Satan" (2 Cor. 2:11).

Let's explore the stages of what I now call "Satan's setup."

Stage 1: Overwhelm the culture with sin

Satan has always used sin as his primary means of destruction. It's fairly easy for him actually, because sin is like a spinning top. Once it's spun into motion, it continues to spiral out of control without any more intervention. Given enough time, the outcome of sin is always death (Rom. 6:23).

The Creation story illustrates most clearly how Satan uses sin to accomplish his goal to steal and kill and destroy. Adam and Eve were made to enjoy eternal life in the perfect world that God had established for them. This was a place of incredible freedom and delight. In fact, they could do and have just about anything they wanted, except one thing. God instructed that they not eat from the tree of the knowledge of good and evil (Gen. 2:17).

Of course, Satan saw the tree as the perfect tool for temptation. In the right moment he presented himself to Eve with a question: "Did God say, 'You shall not eat from any tree in the garden'?" (Gen. 3:1). This question fixed Eve's mind upon the very thing that she was forbidden to consume. Eve knew God had warned that if they ate of the tree, they would certainly die. But Satan countered with a lie. "You will not die," he sneered. He then directed Eve's eyes to the tree so that she saw that it was beautiful, with fruit that appeared luscious. It even seemed to promise wisdom (v. 6).

With Eve's mind and eyes now captivated by the tree's deceptive grandeur, it was all over. She and her husband became overwhelmed by its lure, and they took the bait. Sin's effects were then instantly seen. The first couple could no longer enjoy eternal life in God's presence, but they died a spiritual death that day. And from then on, the Bible reveals, "death spread to everyone" (Rom. 5:12, NLT).

Satan isn't particularly inventive. In fact, he has no real creative power. Therefore, he can only use the same tactics over and over, albeit in unique ways. His strategy against you and me today is the same as it was against Adam and Eve, but on a much larger scale.

Paul prophesied that the last days would be distressing times. People will be "lovers of pleasure rather than lovers of God," he foretold (2 Tim. 3:4). Then he described the state of the culture that would produce such people. They will be "overwhelmed by their sins and swayed by all kinds of desires," he warned (v. 6).

Overwhelmed by sin. This is what the Lord revealed to me is the first stage in Satan's strategy. To be overwhelmed means to be so bombarded by something until it defeats you. And this is precisely how Satan uses sin today in order to destroy us. From the moment we were born, Satan set us up for failure. He did it by inundating our world with so much filth and perversion that it's virtually inescapable. The result is that we live at a time when sin seems normal and righteousness seems strange.

Think about just how pervasive it is. Nearly every magazine in the grocery store checkout line blares some indecent headline. Songs piped into public venues, much less our personal earbuds, all glorify death, anger, and sex. A multibillion-dollar pornography industry targets each of us on our mobile phones every day. We could go on and on. With this much energy put into bombarding our lives with junk, Satan has made it almost inevitable that we fall…over and over again.

Stage 2: Sway with desires

Most of us know all too well the difficulties of going on a diet that restricts what we eat. It doesn't take hardly a day on such a regimen before the food we're supposed to avoid begins to consume our minds. If it's chocolate that you're trying to conquer, then it suddenly seems as if chocolate is everywhere. And you can almost count on it: The moment you begin your diet, a coworker will have a sudden burst of kindness and bring in the most delectable dessert tray he or she never thought of when you weren't watching your weight. If you're not radical about looking away, you eventually justify just a bite, or worse, give in to all-out indulgence.

Satan is like this coworker, although not so well meaning. He directs our attention to the things we know we should stay away from and makes it all look so attractive. He uses the lure of a good feeling or taste, the promise of wisdom, financial security, or even escape from reality. Then, just as he did with

Eve, he lies to us. "This won't be so bad," he says. And before he can finish his lie, we give it a taste.

The overwhelming culture of sin that Satan set up against us is designed to keep our minds in this place at all times. This is crucial to his strategy because he knows that where the mind goes, the man follows. We'll discuss more about the particulars of this in forthcoming chapters. But suffice it to say, what we put before our eyes and our ears eventually influences our thinking, which in turn influences our behaviors. Before long we're consumed with the pleasures of the flesh until we can't get away from what we know is wrong.

This is what Paul meant by a people "swayed by all kinds of desires" (2 Tim. 3:6). Satan intends that we become so addicted to sin that we're led like animals on a leash from one regretful experience to the next.

Stage 3: Taunt with accusations

By definition a *setup* is "a scheme or a trick intended to incriminate someone."[3] And that's the end result of Satan's setup. He overwhelms us with sin, leads us from one regretful experience to the next, and then heaps on guilt and shame. "Look what you've done," he taunts! As you read from my story in the Introduction, this is precisely what he insistently whispered to me, and it almost took me down.

Still, it's nothing new. Using accusations is his age-old trick from the Garden of Eden. Notice that before their sin, Adam and Eve only had knowledge of good. But with their fall, they suddenly possessed knowledge of evil. *Knowledge* is just another word for awareness, and *evil* is the same as immorality. After Satan led the first couple into the first sin, they immediately possessed something they never had before: knowledge of their immorality, or in other words, guilt.

With this newfound feeling of guilt Adam and Eve grew

strangely quiet. In fact, they felt so ashamed that they couldn't bear to be seen by God. Feeling unworthy of His love and His presence, they hid and isolated themselves from their Creator (Gen. 3:7–8).

Guilt has a way of muzzling and isolating. I've felt this in my life, and I'm sure you have too. When I start to get quiet, it's time to ask me what's going on. Often these extended "quiet times" are a result of condemnation. Somehow I get convinced that I have to pay for my sin with a period of seclusion and silence. This is precisely where the devil wants you. He'll tell you that you've messed up too much and are therefore too far beyond God's love or His use.

It's all an extremely potent plan because Satan knows that the greatest hindrance to being used by God is to believe that God can't use you. What could be more destructive to people whose greatest fears are living lives that don't make a difference?

A Prevailing Plan

Satan's tactics may be slick and seductive, but his strategies aren't the only plans in place for your life. After the warning Jesus gave regarding the devil's mission "to steal and kill and destroy," He concluded with an encouragement about God's intentions for you and me.

I came that they may have life, and have it abundantly.
—JOHN 10:10

Jesus's words completely contrast Satan's plan from God's. One is death. The other is life. And the life that Jesus came to bring is extremely rich. *Life* here is translated from the Greek word *zoe*, which is an existence that's fresh, powerful, and full of vitality. Jesus later links the word with "resurrection." "I am the resurrection and the life," He assures. "Those who believe in me, even though they die, will live" (John 11:25).

Indeed, Jesus came to bring a resurrected life. But resurrection involves two events: death and restoration. When Christ says He came to bring life, He means that He came so that we would die to our old selves with our fleshly impulses and be restored into something powerful and new.

Even greater, Jesus guarantees this resurrected life in abundance—full and overflowing. Eighteenth-century Bible commentator Matthew Henry described the abundant life in this way: "Something more, something better; *life with advantage!*"[4]

> **advantage**—a condition or circumstance that puts one in a favorable or superior position[5]

"Life with advantage" involves being in a superior position over Satan, which is exactly why it's advantageous. The abundant life that Jesus offers includes power over Satan instead of Satan having power over you. It's a life made new and made right, not haunted by the past, but made as if the past never happened. That's an exciting plan! This too was all set up well before you were born. In fact, as you'll discover later in this book, God's plan was established at the foundations of the earth.

If you feel overwhelmed by sin or beat down by the devil's torment, know this: God's plans always prevail, even in the face of what seems like a hopeless situation. God is passionate about pursuing you—into the darkest places if He has to—in order to bring you to the place of victory where you'll find this new life. The purpose of this book is to help show the way.

Chapter 2

THE PROFILE OF
THE ACCUSER

DRAW ME A PROFILE OF SATAN. WHAT DOES HE look like to you? What does he do? From where does he do it? The classic image—the one you'll likely draw—is a red guy with horns and a pitchfork. You'll probably tell me that he orchestrates all the evil in the world from his command center in hell.

I'm not sure where it came from, but this pervasive image of Satan is nothing more than myth. The devil is not red with horns and a pitchfork. And while he does orchestrate evil, he doesn't do it from hell. Surprising to most people, the Bible doesn't say that Satan's home is in hell or that he's ever been there at all. Quite the opposite, actually. Jesus revealed that hell is the place *prepared* to *destroy* Satan and his demons (Matt. 25:41), not their home. The devil will not see hell until after his final rebellion at the end of time when he is thrown into the lake of fire (Rev. 20:7–10).

This obviously begs the question: If the devil isn't in hell, where is he, and what is he doing? According to Scripture, he's in one of two places doing one of two things: on earth or in heaven, opposing or accusing.

The Adversary

The Bible reveals that the first place Satan spends his time is roaming the earth searching for people to attack.

> Discipline yourselves, keep alert. Like a roaring lion your adversary the devil prowls around, looking for someone to devour.
> —1 PETER 5:8

Like most names in Scripture, "Satan" is more than a name; it's a job description. It means "one who opposes or blocks." This is why Peter referred to him as *"your* adversary." Let me emphasize Peter's words: Satan is your personal adversary. He's your greatest opponent. We've all seen man-to-man defense in the game of basketball. Picture yourself moving about the court as the devil hovers, intimidating you, maybe even with under-the-breath comments: "You can't make this. You're no good." As you try harder to concentrate on the goal, he moves in, almost breathing in your face, all to make you fumble or miss your shot. Now you have a better picture of how the devil works as your adversary. He's against everything about you and tries to block every attempt for you to grow closer to God.

People often exclaim, "The devil is stupid!" I've said it before. Maybe you have too. While I understand that we say this in order to minimize Satan and to make him seem less threatening, he isn't stupid. A stupid person doesn't easily pull off the genocide of 5.5 million of God's people, as he did through Hitler. A stupid person doesn't succeed in murdering 12 people and injuring another 70, as he did in the Aurora, Colorado, theater massacre. A stupid person doesn't set up an entire culture to be overwhelmed with sin so that the best of us fall to temptation. Too many of us view Satan as a mere nuisance that causes slight inconveniences like heavy traffic, a flat tire, or a toothache. He's not that innocent!

Peter likened Satan to "a roaring lion" that prowls about looking for someone to eat up. As your adversary, Satan spends time studying you, and he knows your weaknesses. On the prowl, he follows you and waits for a weak moment, which is his moment to pounce. Lust. Offense. Anger. Pride. Jealousy. You name it. Whatever you're most susceptible to—your signature sin—that's what he launches against you at his most opportune time.

The Accuser

"It's been one of those days," Holley confessed on her blog. "The kind I wish I could just rewind and begin again." All in one day she had messed up, made mistakes, fallen down, and by the evening, she felt pretty small. "I wonder if God can use still me," she questioned. "Even more, if he still *wants* to use me."

Of course, Holley knew the answer, but still she needed the affirmation of her husband. "Do you think God wants to get rid of me?" she whispered to him. Without hesitation, he replied, "No, but I think the devil does."

Holley recounted that her husband's simple statement changed the day. She wrote, "I recognize the *'you're not good enough, how could you, you've let everyone down'* voice for who it truly belongs to. Not my Advocate but my accuser."[1]

What Holley experienced is the second of Satan's loves—accusing. In addition to roaming the earth, the Bible says he spends his time in heaven, constantly going back and forth before the throne of God making accusations against you and me.

> For the accuser of our brothers and sisters has been
> thrown down to earth—the one who accuses them
> before our God day and night.
>
> —REVELATION 12:10, NLT

Satan stands before the Lord like a prosecuting attorney before a judge, filing claim after claim of how you tripped up, did wrong, and are no longer worthy of God's grace. He enters heaven day and night to deceptively appeal to God's righteousness to try and convince God that He can't use you.

As I mentioned in the previous chapter, Satan's schemes are nothing new. This is exactly what he did with Job.

> One day the heavenly beings came to present themselves before the LORD, and Satan also came among them. The LORD said to Satan, "Where have you come from?" Satan answered the LORD, "From going to and fro on the earth, and from walking up and down on it."
>
> —JOB 1:6–7

Satan spent his time on earth roaming and scoping out someone to devour. Then he came before the Lord's throne to make his accusations. When God brought his attention to Job, a man who, by the Lord's own admission, was "blameless and upright" (v. 8), Satan went to work to devour. Satan took Job's property, children, and health, and then he appeared before the Lord to make his accusations. In the next chapter we'll explore the specific way Satan attacked Job, but for now, suffice it to say that Satan's two roles—adversary and accuser—were responsible for Job's near destruction.

Satan doesn't just make his accusations in heaven, though. You and I feel the heat of his prosecution just about every day. I believe that he goes to heaven to try and get God's attention. When God doesn't listen, he scurries back to earth to find an audience. All too often you and I happily entertain his case. This is the bulk of the spiritual warfare that we feel. The devil attacks, causes us to fall, takes our failures to God, and then brings them back to us. Unfortunately the devil doesn't have to try too hard. As it did with Holley, the smallest reminder of wrongdoing can beat us down and make us believe we're no longer of any use to God.

The Light Bearer

You're in a battle for your destiny! As with facing any opponent, the better understanding you have of your rival, the better are your chances of victory. The devil knows who you are, where you came from, and what pushes your buttons, and he works to use it all against you. We should know the same about him so that we might have better insight into how to face and overcome his attacks.

The prophet Ezekiel was given a glimpse into the origins of Satan. In a vision he saw the devil in Eden, not as the sinister serpent, but as the most beautiful angel who was the mirror of God's perfection.

> You were the signet of perfection, full of wisdom and perfect in beauty. You were in Eden, the garden of God; every precious stone was your covering, carnelian, chrysolite, and moonstone, beryl, onyx, and jasper, sapphire, turquoise, and emerald; and worked in gold were your settings and your engravings. On the day that you were created they were prepared. With an anointed cherub as guardian I placed you; you were on the holy mountain of God; you walked among the stones of fire. You were blameless in your ways from the day that you were created, until iniquity was found in you.
>
> —EZEKIEL 28:12–15

It's hard to fathom, but Satan was once the "signet of perfection"; that is, the mold of perfection by which all other perfection was compared against. Besides the Lord Himself, nothing appeared wiser or more beautiful. Get the picture: Satan modeled the best that the Lord had created.

Ezekiel intentionally described Satan's elaborate clothing as adorned with precious stones. Today there are dozens of these stones, otherwise known as gems. While in Eden Satan was robed with them all. Just imagine the beauty. He shimmered with chrysolite, a greenish-yellow, light-reflecting gemstone. He glowed with moonstone, known for its magnificent aura that appears from deep within. He radiated with the unparalleled green of an emerald.[2]

The stones used to describe Satan's robe are some of the most exquisite and rare gems known today. Most are prism-like and refract and reflect, and so their beauty is only appreciated in light. Imagine these gems in the presence of the One who is the purest of light. Anyone adorned with such a robe would radiate this presence in the most astonishing of ways. This is why Satan was once known as Lucifer, which means "light bearer" (Isa. 14:12, KJV). What Satan was given was a robe that bore God's light and was a brilliant reflection of God Himself. Truly, covered in this robe, Satan was covered in God's best and was the mirror of God's perfection.

The Wannabe Celebrity in Heaven

> Your heart was proud because of your beauty; you corrupted your wisdom for the sake of your splendor.
> —EZEKIEL 28:17

Notice what Ezekiel said: "*your* beauty...*your* wisdom...*your* splendor." What was meant to be a gift from God to reflect God's presence, Lucifer eventually considered his own. I can just imagine him in this glimmering fashion, strutting around as the celebrity of heaven, marveling, "Look at *my* beauty. Admire *my* light." These are terms of worship, which is what he came to desire. This marked the beginning of his end. At the height of his arrogance he exclaimed:

> I will ascend to heaven; I will raise my throne above the stars of God; I will sit on the mount of assembly on the heights of Zaphon; I will ascend to the tops of the clouds, *I will make myself like the Most High.*
> —ISAIAH 14:13–14,
> emphasis added

Lucifer, puffed up with pride, attempted to turn heaven's attention away from God and to himself. But there can be only one celebrity in heaven. There's only One whose glory is to be celebrated throughout the universe. This is the Lord God, creator of the heavens, the earth, and all that is in them, which includes Lucifer and the angels (Exod. 20:11). God alone is the famous One.

With his five "I wills" Lucifer sealed his fate. His robe was taken from him, and with it the entire splendor that he so much enjoyed. The Lord cast him down to earth (Ezek. 28:17), where he became "Satan," the adversary to God and everything that God loves. He still revels to be seen as glorious, which is why he masquerades as the angel of light that he once was (2 Cor. 11:14). But there is no light in him, for now he is the signet—the model—of darkness.

Many ask the question: "Why did God create Satan?" This is a fair question, but you must understand that God didn't create *Satan.* God created *Lucifer,* the light bearer, as heaven's instrument to reflect His glory and display His splendor. Lucifer was to be a mirror so that whoever looked at him saw the Lord Himself. But in his pride Lucifer devised to usurp

27

God, and so Lucifer himself created the prince of darkness that we know as Satan.

Why Satan Hates You

Obviously the devil is rather upset with God. But why does Satan take it out on you and me? Why does he vehemently oppose God's creation and everything that they do? Ultimately it's because he can't defeat God. And this is crucial to understand: Spiritual warfare is never Satan against God, as if they are coequals. No, the devil is so much smaller and therefore must pick on people more his own size, which are you and me. Also, the Bible reveals that God favors humankind more than all of creation (Gen. 1:28–30) and has given us things that, as you'll see below, pose a formidable threat to Satan in four powerful ways.

1. You remind the devil of who he can't be.

Satan is an extremely jealous character. All of his five "I wills" were aimed at becoming the most powerful and most worshiped—to be like the Most High. He wants to be God, but the job is not available. And when someone wants something badly enough, but can't have it, he becomes extremely bitter.

When God spoke people into existence, He said, "Let us make humankind in our image, according to our likeness" (Gen. 1:26). In the next verse He confirmed His handiwork:

> So God created humankind in his image, in the image of God he created them; male and female he created them.
>
> —Genesis 1:27

What Genesis describes is nothing short of astonishing. You and I resemble God! Sure, because of sin, we may be a distorted image, but we bear His qualities nonetheless.

All of creation is God's and is therefore special and should be honored. Still, nothing but humanity can claim to be made in God's image. Take a look. Prior to the creation of people, the Lord uses "Let there be…" or "Let there bring forth…" as His means to create. To create animals, for instance, He spoke, "Let the *earth bring forth* living creatures of every kind" (v. 24, emphasis added). Notice that it's out of the earth that animals were created. Humans, however, were created out of the image of God.

When Satan sees a tree, banana, elephant, dog, or bird, he doesn't necessarily see God, and he isn't too threatened. But when he sees you or me, he gets a potent reminder of God and who he can never be! We're certainly not God, but we're much closer than Satan is—and of that he's tremendously envious. So his scheme is to destroy anything that reminds him of God.

2. You crush his head.

We see from Genesis that the Lord created humankind to have dominion over the creation (Gen. 1:26). We were intended to maintain authority over all the creatures upon the earth and in the sky. But Satan schemed against Adam and Eve and stole the authority that was rightfully ours. In that moment the devil thought he'd won a mighty victory. If he couldn't be the king of heaven, he'd be the ruler of the earth.

With the punishment for the first sin the Lord pronounced a curse upon the devil and forewarned him of his future.

> I will put enmity between you and the woman, and between your offspring and hers; he will strike your head, and you will strike his heel.
> —Genesis 3:15

This verse is often used as the first prophecy of Jesus; that is, Jesus is the offspring of the woman (the Virgin Mary) who will provide the ultimate blow to Satan. This is certainly true, but it also speaks of the woman's "offspring." Eve (the woman) is referred to as "the mother of all living" (Gen. 3:20), and *offspring* means children. Here, the devil was cautioned that one day all of God's children would have the ability to strike his head, while he would remain under their feet. Satan was put on notice that his sham authority would be short-lived, and dominion would be returned back to the people of God.

Short-lived it was! Scripture reveals that Jesus came to "destroy the works of the devil" (1 John 3:8). And He gave this same power to you and me.

> See, I have given you authority to tread on snakes and scorpions, and over all the power of the enemy; and nothing will hurt you.
> —LUKE 10:19

Jesus offered authority to "tread on snakes"; in other words, to crush Satan's head—but not just Satan's head. Jesus also promised authority over all the power of the enemy. You don't have to take the temptations, accusations, and lies of Satan. You have power over them and can declare to him, "No more!"

Authority over all the power of the enemy is God's plan for all His children. This is the life of advantage that Jesus promised because it is a life that remains above the schemes of Satan. The devil is scared stiff of anyone who possesses such a life, and so he works tirelessly to keep you from it.

3. You are clothed in something better.

That beautiful robe that Lucifer enjoyed, with its shimmering gems, was meant only to reflect the righteousness of God and draw worship to Him. We know this robe was the source of Lucifer's beauty and perfection, but it was also the reason he became proud. With Lucifer's fall from grace, I believe the Lord tossed that robe out and prepared something much more splendid for those He would later declare worthy to wear it.

> I will greatly rejoice in the LORD, my whole being shall exult in my God; for he has clothed me with the garments of salvation, he has covered me with the robe of righteousness, as a bridegroom decks himself with a garland, and as a bride adorns herself with her jewels.
> —ISAIAH 61:10

Decked with garland and adorned with jewels is how the prophet Isaiah described a robe *made of righteousness* that would be put upon those who have accepted the Lord's salvation. The robe that Lucifer once enjoyed shimmered and glimmered as it *reflected* God's light, but it was never considered *righteousness* itself.

Paul wrote that we are the righteousness of God in Christ Jesus (2 Cor. 5:21). This means that those of us who are believers in Jesus are considered *in* Him. It's like stepping into a uniform. We are literally clothed in Christ and His righteousness (Gal. 3:27).

What a tremendous thought! You are wearing Jesus. You're adorned with God's best! The garments the Lord has prepared for you cover anything else you've ever worn. Those dirty clothes with all of the holes and sin stains are no longer seen. Instead, when God looks at you, He sees righteousness and purity. He sees His reflection—Jesus.

Being adorned in Jesus is more spectacular than any amount of precious stones. Precious stones can only reflect light, but Jesus is light!

I am the light of the world. Whoever follows me will
never walk in darkness but will have the light of life.

—JOHN 8:12

In Christ you have the light of life, and this is greater than
anything Satan ever possessed. Jesus assured that those who
have His light would never walk in darkness; that is, they'll be
above the influence of Satan!

4. God loves you.

The church always looks for the newest revelation or the
freshest insight. We want God to reveal something about
Himself that's never been revealed before. Then we think we
are truly spiritual.

Really, though, there's one single revelation that God wants
you to grasp. It's a powerful concept that stands as the foundation of your life, your faith journey, or anything else the
Lord chooses to reveal to you. It's this: God loves you. There's
nothing more profound than the revelation that the Creator
of this vast universe absolutely cherishes you. This is why God
sent Jesus. Because He *so loves you*.

For God so loved the world that he gave his only Son,
so that everyone who believes in him may not perish
but may have eternal life.

—JOHN 3:16

The Lord designed us for close relationship with Him. This
is what Adam and Eve enjoyed in the garden as they walked
and talked with God. That's the kind of relationship the Lord
wants with you and me. But like in any relationship, whether
with a friend or a spouse, the level of intimacy you allow
yourself to enjoy with the other person is a reflection of how
much you perceive that he or she cares about you. Nobody

wants to get closer to someone who's a jerk, is always critical, or even abusive.

I've seen a bumper sticker that says, "Jesus is coming back, and boy, is He mad." Isn't this the pervasive feeling throughout the culture? So many people believe that God is mad at them. And so they hold God at a distance.

The feeling that God is mad at you is possibly the greatest of Satan's lies. If the devil can get you to believe that your failures have made God mad, then he successfully blocks your ability to have the intimate relationship with God that He so desires. And by blocking your relationship with God, the devil steals your potential for joy, healing, and new life.

God is not mad at you. Make no mistake, He despises sin and ungodliness (Rom. 1:18), but He is madly interested in you. Let me convince you: you are created in God's image. God doesn't despise His own image, does He? No, He loves it! Even when we miss the mark, the Bible declares that God still loves us.

> But God proves his love for us in that while we still were sinners Christ died for us.
> —ROMANS 5:8

Speak this aloud until it gets into your soul: "God loves me. God loves *me. God. Loves. Me.*" I promise, you will naturally get closer to God when you take it to heart that He is madly in love with you.

As you grow closer to God, you grow closer to His voice. Suddenly you'll realize that the voice of God drowns out all others. The temptations, accusations, and lies of Satan will lose their influence, and instead you'll hear God's truth and will gain the confidence you need to be powerfully used by Him. This is why Satan's after you. There's nothing more threatening to him than you armed with the confidence that God absolutely loves you and, therefore, *wants* to use you.

Let's move on to the next chapter to explore the specific tactics the devil uses against each of us individually in order to destroy our faith in God's love for us.

Chapter 3

THE DEVIL'S PLAYBOOK

ACHURCH GROUP INVITED ME TO SPEAK ON A TWO-part series during a study of spiritual warfare. To begin, I shared much of what you read in the first chapter, about the dueling plans of Satan versus God and how the devil whispers lies and accusations in order to keep you out of God's abundant life. When I returned for the second session, a lady approached me to share a story that nearly brought me to tears.

"I had an addiction," she immediately confessed, "an addiction to alcohol." She was sure to tell me that her drinking didn't include hard liquor, which is why it was a bit more justifiable to her. "I was a wine connoisseur," she informed. "I very much enjoyed sophisticated red wine…every day." Her enjoyment didn't consist of a couple sips or even a glass, but she consumed a bottle a day. Really, she admitted, the bottle was consuming her. Her addiction cost her about ten to twenty dollars per day. When she would realize how much she was spending, she'd go down in price, maybe to $6 a bottle, but would eventually return to the higher-priced wines, thinking she deserved it.

When her church group began to study spiritual warfare, she decided to put the wine down. As she spoke to me, she was beaming that she hadn't picked up a bottle in two weeks. Of course, she was beginning to save a considerable amount of money, and she even lost ten pounds!

I was very excited for the lady. Two weeks without alcohol is a great start on the road to recovery. But she continued to tell me that her real freedom came when I shared about Satan's playbook. "It was like I saw behind the scenes of how Satan works," she reported. The message awakened her to Satan's common attacks, and she finally became aware of how he was using the addiction in her life to beat her down and make her feel unworthy. Recognizing the works of the enemy set her free!

This lady's testimony really impassioned me to expose Satan's ways. Now some people argue that we shouldn't give too much attention to the work of the devil because we might lose our focus on the goodness of God. Though that's true, remember that Paul instructed us to at least be familiar with Satan's evil schemes, "so that Satan will not outsmart us" (2 Cor. 2:11, NLT).

I don't want to obsess, but I simply want to bring awareness to the devil's common tactics so that you may be able to recognize and ward off his attacks when they happen.

><s>

Satan is not stupid, nor is he weak, but he is predictable. If you look around at those who would say that they are under attack, more often than not the attacks begin in one place and may be put into one of only a few categories. This is what I call his playbook.

playbook—a stock of usual tactics or methods

A playbook is a notebook that contains outlines and plans for certain situations. It may be best known in the world of sports, such as football, where common techniques and vocabulary relating to game plays and team formations are kept and studied. In theater a playbook likely contains a script and acting strategies relating to characters. Even businesses may use a playbook in order to record how the company is to handle certain activities such as a buyout or a merger. Satan's playbook, like all the others, contains the usual tactics he uses to achieve his ends, which we know is to steal and to kill and to destroy.

The Devil's Playground

We must first understand that the most common place Satan makes his starting play is in the mind. This is why it's said that the mind is the devil's playground. He has the most fun tinkering with your thoughts, because he knows that your thoughts are the forerunners to your actions. Because of this, the Bible frequently reminds us to protect the mind above anything else.

> More than anything you guard, protect your mind, for life flows from it.
> —PROVERBS 4:23, CEB

Life flows from your mind. Your mind plays a large part in the course of your life's journey. Other translations say that the mind is the place from which your issues arise (KJV). Isn't this the truth! Think about it: most of the issues you face stem from what you think about. Thoughts have the power to lead you into temptation or hold you captive to things like hopelessness or depression. The lady in the story kept returning to the wine bottle because she kept her mind on the taste and experience of drinking wine. A man who keeps lust on his mind will eventually fall to sexual sin. A teenage girl who constantly compares herself to the airbrushed magazine models will always feel as if she isn't good enough. This is what the Bible teaches—that we live according to our flesh when our minds are set on things of the flesh.

> For those who live according to the flesh set their minds on the things of the flesh, but those who live according to the Spirit set their minds on the things of the Spirit. To set the mind on the flesh is death, but to set the mind on the Spirit is life and peace.
> —ROMANS 8:5–6

Truly, where the mind goes, the man follows. Whatever you feel—confident or insecure, loved or unloved, hopeful or hopeless—it's more than likely a result of thoughts. Satan knows this, which is why he likes to use our minds as his garbage dump to inject his stinkin' thinkin'.

> We destroy every proud obstacle that keeps people from knowing God. We capture their rebellious thoughts and teach them to obey Christ.
> —2 CORINTHIANS 10:5, NLT

Satan devises thoughts to be obstacles to keep you from growing closer to God. Remember, that's what his name means: "one who blocks." His thoughts are described as rebellious because they are in opposition to the truth of God. In other words, Satan comes to speak lies and doubts, most of the time about something God has declared or promised, and your mind does the rest of his dirty work. "What if…," "I can't…," "This will never…," and "Did God say?" will plague you until your entire life is held captive by Satan's schemes.

Play #1: Speak Lies

The Bible says, "There is nothing new under the sun" (Eccles. 1:9), and that's certainly true of Satan's attacks. Jesus revealed the devil has used the same tricks since the beginning of Creation.

> He was a murderer from the beginning and does not stand in the truth, because there is no truth in him. When he lies, he speaks according to his own nature, for he is a liar and the father of lies.
> —JOHN 8:44

How do you know when Satan's lying? According to Jesus, it's when his mouth is moving! Everything the devil speaks is a lie, for he is the father of lies. A lie is simply an untrue statement with the intent to *deceive*. And deception takes place in the mind, which is where we said most of Satan's attacks begin.

Recall again the story of Adam and Eve, which is the story Jesus was likely referring to when he called Satan a murderer and liar from the beginning.

Upon finishing His magnificent work of Creation, God said to the first couple, "See, I have given you every plant yielding seed that is upon the face of all the earth, and every tree with seed in its fruit; you shall have them for food" (Gen. 1:29). As we know, Adam and Eve were allowed to eat of every tree, except the one known as the tree of the knowledge of good and evil (Gen. 2:16–17).

By this time Satan had been kicked out of heaven and was awaiting his opportunity to deceive. When he approached Eve, he came with a dose of doubt. *"Did God say, 'You shall not eat from any tree in the garden'?"* Eve knew God's words and responded accordingly. Satan's next tactic was a bold-faced lie. He said, *"You will not die; for God knows that when you eat of* it your eyes will be opened, and you will be like God, knowing good and evil" (Gen. 3:1–5, emphasis added).

At this point you can imagine that Eve's mind began to spin. "Maybe God is holding back from me. Can I really trust God? Does He really love me?" she likely questioned.

Has your mind ever run down a similar rabbit trail? I know mine has, and so have the minds of many others! It seems like I'm always talking to people who are held back from all that God has for them simply because of the lies of the devil. A lady who suffered from traumatic back injury and pain once confessed to me that for years she resisted going forward in church to have hands laid upon her for healing because she never thought she was good enough. In fact, she thought there were other, more serious issues for God to take care of first. She basically believed that God had a limited supply of miracles, and she didn't want to use one for herself in case someone else needed it more. Perhaps it seems like a nice gesture to prefer others first, but what she believed was a lie, and it held her back. The truth is that God's love and compassion toward you never runs dry. He has enough for you and everyone else on this planet.

> The steadfast love of the LORD never ceases, his mercies never come to an end; they are new every morning; great is your faithfulness. "The LORD is my portion," says my soul, "therefore I will hope in him."
> —LAMENTATIONS 2:22–24

Be encouraged that you can trust God to see you through whatever challenges life throws at you. His love never ceases toward you. He's not holding back any good thing from you (Ps. 84:11). If you haven't yet received what you're praying for, it's because God is working on something better. In fact, even as you read this, the Lord is whipping up a brand-new batch of love, compassion, hope, and healing, *just for you.*

Satan wants you to doubt all of this, which is why lies are the first tactics in his playbook. Lies are his scheme to keep you from all that God has for you. Some of the other lies that you should recognize are:

- ◊ You'll never overcome your sin.
- ◊ You'll always be rejected.
- ◊ Nobody loves you, not even God.
- ◊ You can't do anything right.
- ◊ Your life is hopeless.
- ◊ Bad things will always happen to you.
- ◊ You can't trust anyone.
- ◊ You're too dirty to be used by God.

Play #2: Overwhelm With Guilt and Shame

With a lie Satan penetrated the hearts of Adam and Eve. They possessed knowledge of good *and* evil and an awareness of their immorality, which is why they suddenly saw themselves naked and hid from God. What the first couple experienced was the first guilt and shame.

> **guilt**—a bad feeling caused by knowing or thinking that you have done something bad or wrong

> **shame**—a painful emotion caused by consciousness of guilt, shortcoming, or impropriety

Guilt and shame are very similar to each other. Each is rooted in the feeling that you have done something wrong. But there are a couple very important distinctions. Guilt is always felt first. It's the immediate voice: "I have done something wrong." You should know that an initial feeling of guilt isn't always wrong. Perhaps it's part of the Spirit's conviction, which is often what's necessary for repentance. But it becomes very crippling if it persists after you've repented.

Persistent, unchecked guilt eventually turns into shame. It's the devil's follow-up tactic, and it's very potent. Whereas guilt says, "I *have done* something wrong," shame says, "I *am* something wrong."[1] Shame is the identification with the devil's lie: "I am unworthy; I am dirty; I am alone; I am unloved; I am hopeless." Shame is what Adam and Eve experienced when they realized they were naked. This is what they attempted to cover up with their own fig leaves; this is why they hid from God.

Certainly guilt and shame are the devil's logical next steps after he's tempted you into sin. But other times it's not a result of anything you did wrong, but of the circumstances he's put you in. It's another part of Satan's setup that I spoke about in chapter 1. To explain, I'm going to bear my soul to you and reveal some things from my past that I've only shared with one or two very close friends.

In my elementary years I was extremely shy, almost debilitating so. When I was in kindergarten and first grade, my teachers thought I had a reading problem. As a result, several times a week they'd separate me from the rest of class to join a handful of other students for extra help with reading. My parents thought this was curious because they observed that I could read perfectly fine at home.

By the time I was in second grade, the teachers finally realized the root of the problem. When they'd call on me to read in class, I'd freeze, and so what they thought was a reading problem was actually timidity.

My shyness didn't only affect reading, but it also severely inhibited my ability to make friends or excel at much of anything, especially athletically. Because of this, I was misunderstood by most of my classmates and became an outcast at school. Things that most kids live for, such as recess and PE class, I dreaded every day. It was embarrassing to have no one to play with on the playground or to be picked last for the team.

I tried to hide the fact that I was an outcast. When we'd have class parties or parent days, I'd never tell my mom or dad, hoping they wouldn't show up. I remember them feeling hurt because they thought I was ashamed of them. The truth was that I was ashamed of myself. I never wanted them to see me with no friends, in such a pitiful place.

"Why am I so shy? Why does no one want to be my friend? Why can't I kick the ball as well? It must be because *I am something wrong*," I thought. I became ashamed of myself. As time went on, like Adam and Eve, I tried to cover up my shame with a variety of my own figs leaves, including overachieving, perfectionism, maintaining only distant relationships, and avoiding certain types of situations. The devil set me up to be shackled by shame so that I couldn't experience the free life that Jesus died to give.

Play #3: Steal Their Identity

Identity theft is all the rage these days. In fact, the US government cites stolen identities as one of the top consumer complaints every year. According to a study done by Javelin Strategy and Research, more than 12 million people were victims of this crime in 2012.[2] Of course, those affected often spend tens of thousands of dollars in attempts to restore their identity, which is why almost every insurance company now offers some sort extra policy for added protection.

The rate of identity theft is actually much higher than the

US government reports. In fact, most people that I know have all suffered from a stolen identity at one point in their life—at least spiritually speaking. Identity theft was first Satan's idea and is his greatest scheme! It's precisely the goal of his lies and shame. Instead of you seeing yourself in the image of God, Satan wants you to see yourself in the image of your problems, struggles, what someone else said about you, or whatever situation you're in. Then he'll come in with whispers questioning your status before God. This is play #3 in his playbook. The devil wants you to be identified by his whispers instead of what God says about you.

In Scripture Job is a fitting example of someone who felt the tension between God's words and Satan's whispers.

The story of Job opens with a declaration of Job's identity: "There was once a man in the land of Uz whose name was Job. That man was blameless and upright, one who feared God and turned away from evil" (Job 1:1).

After a brief description of Job's family the story enters a heavenly courtroom scene where Job's identity is questioned. Here, Satan appears before the Lord, probably to make his usual accusations. Then God brings Satan's attention to Job. "Have you considered my servant Job?" God appears to brag. "There is no one like him on the earth, a blameless and upright man who fears God and turns away from evil" (v. 8.)

With a bit of arrogance, it seems, Satan asks permission of God to test Job, and God permits it, as long as Job's life isn't touched. Job 1 and 2 detail the devil's attempts to steal Job's possessions, children, and his health.

Close friends and family are always first to notice our hardships. Job's friends were no different. They observed his great suffering and came to his side to accompany him, but for seven days they didn't utter a word (Job 2:13)—that is, until the devil starting whispering his words.

In the night Job's best friend Eliphaz heard a voice that changed everything.

> Now a word came stealing to me, my ear received the whisper of it. Amid thoughts from visions of the night, when deep sleep falls on mortals, dread came upon me, and trembling, which made all my bones shake. A spirit glided past my face; the hair of my flesh bristled. It stood still, but I could not discern its appearance. A form was before my eyes; there was silence, then I heard a voice: "Can mortals be righteous before God? Can human beings be pure before their Maker?"
> —JOB 4:12–17

Eliphaz reported that a spirit began to speak to him in the night, which caused him much fear and trembling. Various scholars have attempted to identify this spirit. Some claim it was an angel; others think it was God Himself. But God doesn't cause dread, nor does He put His own words into question. Previously God had declared Job to be righteous and pure. But this spirit questioned that very identity. This was not the work of God, but of Satan himself!

You can almost hear the devil's sinister, instigating voice: "Can mortals be righteous before God? Can human beings be pure before their Maker?" It's the same tactic he used with Eve to cause her to doubt God's words.

In the case with Job, Satan posed these questions to steal Job's identity. Job's friend was so convinced by Satan's questions that he broke his silence to declare Job a sinner.

> Stop and think! Do the innocent die? When have the upright been destroyed? My experience shows that those who plant trouble and cultivate evil will harvest the same.
> —JOB 4:7–8, NLT

Satan had won a victory. No longer was Job recognized by the identity that God had declared, but by the one Satan had planted through his whispers.

The question Satan asked is an important one to consider. Ultimately he whispers the same question to you and me just about every day. Can we be righteous and pure? In other words, are we worthy of God's love? Certainly we aren't worthy based upon our own merits. The Bible asserts that we are all unrighteous because "all have sinned and fall short of the glory of God" (Rom. 3:23). Yet for those of us who have made Jesus our Lord and Savior, God *declares* us righteous.

> For our sake he made him to be sin who knew no sin, so
> that in him we might become the righteousness of God.
> —2 CORINTHIANS 5:21

So what do we make of Satan's question? Can human beings be pure before their Maker? Yes, but only *if* God declares them as such. Know that you and I are *nothing* by ourselves, but we are *everything* in Christ.

Understanding my true identity in Christ was crucial to breaking the false identity that I had built up from years of rejection. I had to come to realize that I'm not my past, my struggles, or what anyone else has ever said about me. God's Word is my ultimate reality, and He calls me righteous, loved, and accepted. This is your true identity too, and don't let any accusations or whispers from Satan make you believe otherwise.

Section II

THE PLACE OF VICTORY

Chapter 4

THE NOOSE OR THE NAILS

LOOK WHAT YOU'VE DONE! GOD CAN'T USE YOU!
Shut it all down!" Remember those three accusations
the devil launched at me? These are the whispers I heard
every day throughout the next week as I awoke, drove in to the
office, or put my head on my pillow at night. I remember my
heart pounding from anxiety as reminders of my sins tumbled
through my mind. I was afraid to answer phone calls or look
at new e-mails in fear that it might be bad news. I soon learned
these feelings were the evil forebodings mentioned in Proverbs.

> All the days of the desponding and afflicted are made
> evil [by anxious thoughts and forebodings], but he
> who has a glad heart has a continual feast [regardless
> of circumstances].
> —PROVERBS 15:15, AMP

Forebodings are fearful apprehensions, a sense that something bad will happen. This is a trap that Satan uses to keep
people from boldness. His accusations only bring fear so that
negativity, doubt, and worry rule the mind rather than faith.
That's precisely what I felt. Satan was using my mind as his

garbage dump to inject his lies and feelings of guilt and shame for things from the past. My mind was so gripped with fear that I began to expect the sky could fall on me at any moment.

Sadly, many people live this way in everyday life. Using evidence from the past, Satan launches the lie that God is mad, and they are therefore subject to His punishments. So, rather than expect His goodness in circumstances, they expect His wrath. "Whatever can go wrong will go wrong" is the mantra. A simple test at the doctor's office incites fears of the deadliest diagnosis. A call to speak with the boss is a sure sign of being canned. If children are late coming home, it's assumed that the worst has happened.

When you give in to these forebodings, you allow yourself to become a prisoner to fear and are held back from what God offers for your future. Certainly this isn't the free life that Jesus died to give, but rather it's Satan's way of overwhelming you with guilt and shame in order to silence your voice and kill your destiny.

The Judas Story

We've seen how Satan uses lies and accusations to destroy people. Lying to Adam and Eve, he stole their dominion and instituted death into God's perfect creation. Whispers and accusations stole Job's identity and just about destroyed him. Though these are bad enough, the story of Judas perhaps best illustrates the place Satan wants to take us.

Judas Iscariot, otherwise known as the Betrayer, might possibly be the most hated person in Scripture. His name always appears last in any list of the disciples, likely indicating the repulse the Gospel writers held toward him. For many of us just the mention of his name evokes disgust. Judas represents the worst of the worst. He's the intimate enemy—the brother or sister, close friend, business colleague—who betrays your trust, steals your money, or stabs you in the back. We all have at least one person in our lives who reminds us of Judas.

To Jesus, he was one of His twelve most trusted companions—so trusted, in fact, that he kept and controlled the ministry money bag (John 13:29). But as we know all too well, even the closest followers of Jesus aren't immune to the devil's schemes. Scripture recounts that Satan entered Judas and influenced him to give Jesus up to the chief priests and temple police for His arrest (Luke 22:3–6). The traitor gave in to his lust for greed and betrayed his Savior for thirty silver coins.

To make matters worse, Judas outright denied what he had done. When Jesus forewarned His disciples that one would betray him, Judas retorted, "Surely not I, Rabbi?" (Matt. 26:25). But he surely did. Imagine the scene. Jesus prays in the Garden of Gethsemane with so much agony regarding what will take place that His own blood swells to the surface and begins to trickle as sweat through His pores. Heavy on His heart are the events that have yet to unfold in order that the plan of salvation may be complete.

The marching sounds of a crowd inching closer and closer disrupt His prayers. Swords and clubs shuffle and clang alongside soldier's belts as they creep their way in toward Jesus. From out of the distance, almost like the sun peaking over the horizon at daybreak, Jesus catches His first glimpse of His betrayer in action. It's Judas, leading a mob of angry priests and elders. He can almost read the words from Judas's lips: "The one I will kiss is *the man*" (Matt. 26:48, emphasis added).

The man. Is this all Jesus had become to Judas? It sounds so cold upon the lips of one personally selected by Christ as an apostle from the beginning. He was among those given authority over the works of the devil, with power to cure disease and sickness (Matt. 10:1). Judas stood beside Jesus in some of the most intimate moments as He revealed parables, calmed a storm, and restored a girl to life.

But eventually these works became familiar, and Jesus was just a man to Judas. It's the temptation we all face. What was once holy becomes common. And when that's the case, it's easy for Satan to convince us of anything. It's too easy to betray Jesus when He's no longer Lord but just a mere man in your life.

Judas would betray Him with a kiss, which in those days might be likened to our handshake; it was an act of greeting and companionship. Often it was the means of showing honor and respect. Sometimes the kiss is referred to as a kiss of peace. But the kiss of Judas was anything but honorable or peaceable. Jesus was keenly aware of what was about to happen, but true to His word, He turned His cheek toward Judas to receive what I'm sure was the most lifeless and disgracing kiss ever known to man. With this callous act the Son of God was handed over for the highest and most gruesome means of Roman execution—crucifixion on a cross.

The Way of the Noose

How could one so close to the Lord to do something like this? Like Adam and Eve and many others before him, Judas was the victim of his desires. Scripture portrays him as a man with affection for money. He cared so deeply for possessions that he got upset when Mary anointed Jesus's feet with a pound of expensive perfume. "Why was this perfume not sold for three hundred denarii and the money given to the poor?" Judas probed (John 12:5).

Money was his weakness, and Satan knew it. According to coin experts, the amount Judas was offered to give up Jesus was about the value of a small farm in those days.[1] For a man with a love for money, the temptation was significant. Before we cast judgment as to how someone could do such a thing, let's put it in modern terms. The amount Judas was offered is the equivalent of a new house in a nice neighborhood or at least several high-end luxury cars. I know I've betrayed Jesus for so much less.

When it came time for Judas to make his deal for Jesus's arrest, I'm sure he couldn't conceive of his sin's consequences. Do any of us ever see sin's effects played out in the moment? Satan's lures can be so tantalizing that we're nearly blinded by its instant gratification and tricked to believe, "This won't be so bad." Sadly I've even said to myself, "I'll just ask for forgiveness later." But after the deed is done, Satan swoops in with constant reminders of just how bad it is. "It's so bad," he'll tell you, "that you're worthless to God."

When Judas felt the weight of his sin, he became filled with sorrow. The Bible actually says that he repented. He returned those thirty silver coins to the priests and elders, confessing, "I have sinned by betraying innocent blood" (Matt. 27:4). By this time, however, it was too late. The religious leaders had what they wanted, and there was no turning back.

In this moment Satan also had Judas right where he wanted him, so filled with guilt and shame from his actions that he could barely stand to live. Imagine the condemnation he must have felt after giving up the Son of God for death. Imagine the whispers he must have heard: "You've done the unthinkable. God will never forgive you." Judas would surrender to Satan's voice one final time. Tormented by accusations, and by what I'm sure was an overwhelming sense of worthlessness, Judas ran away and hanged himself in a place called the potter's field.

The potter's field was given its name because of its potter's clay, which was useless for agriculture and, therefore, a suitable site for a graveyard. The chief priests used the money they received from the betrayal of Jesus to purchase this land for the burial of strangers. The priests renamed the field to *Akeldama*, an Aramaic word meaning "Field of Blood."

"Field of Blood" is a fitting description for the place Satan had led Judas. It was a place of uselessness, a place for strangers, and a place of death. Satan's accusations convinced Judas that he was no longer useful to God. He convinced him that because God wouldn't forgive him, he was a stranger to God. He led Judas down a path to a noose whereby he was hanged from the very ropes with which he was bound.

I certainly don't intend to sugarcoat Judas's image, or even remove his responsibility in the death of Jesus. But his story completely depicts Satan's setup from beginning to end. Satan studied Judas's weaknesses and used them to lure him into sin. Once Judas took Satan's bait, he hanged himself with guilt and condemnation. With this, Satan achieved his goal to steal and kill and destroy.

The Way of the Cross

Meanwhile in Jerusalem, Jesus endured trial after trial by those seeking to silence Him. The religious leaders filed various charges, including blasphemy and treason, and eventually incited the public to demand that the Roman government sentence Jesus to death by crucifixion.

Undoubtedly crucifixion was the most horrible form of Roman execution, typically reserved only for slaves and the worst kinds of criminals. Citizens of Rome could not be subjected to such cruelty. Those sentenced to death on a cross first endured pre-crucifixion torture, which often included flogging, burning, and various means of bone-chilling mutilation. Once he was sufficiently beaten, the criminal was made to carry a cross to the site of the execution, where even more tremendous torture and humiliation awaited as he was affixed to a wooden cross by nails.

How could Jesus, a perfect, sinless man, be found guilty and sentenced to such an atrocious execution? Ultimately it wasn't blasphemy, treason, or any of the false charges the religious leaders brought against him. Jesus was found guilty because of the disease that has plagued humanity since Adam and Eve fell in the Garden of Eden—sin. As it did to all the others before Him, sin led Jesus to His death too.

> He personally carried our sins in his body on the cross
> so that we can be dead to sin and live for what is right.
> —1 PETER 2:24, NLT

Unlike all the others, though, Jesus wasn't led to His death because of His own sin; He was led to His death by your sins, my sins, and the sins of the entire world. Jesus had taken so much sin upon Himself that Scripture says He actually became sin (2 Cor. 5:21). It must have been the most horrendous sight on earth.

The Son of God afflicted with sin was Satan's delight, and it appeared Jesus would share the same fate as Judas. With guilt Satan led Judas down a road to hang from a tree. With the guilt of the world he would lead Jesus down a road to hang on a tree. The road marked for Jesus would be a path of intense suffering, a path known as the *Via Dolorosa*—the Way of the Cross.

If silencing Jesus was the goal, the Way of the Cross was the surest bet to its achievement. In fact, the Roman cross at the end of that road was the ultimate means of silencing. A. W. Tozer insightfully recognized, "It knew no compromise; it never made concessions. It won all of its arguments by killing its opponents and silencing him for good."[2]

The devil knew the scripture that stated, "Anyone hung on a tree is under God's curse" (Deut. 21:23). So as Jesus endured the tremendous thrashing along this path and found His place upon the tree, Satan smirked, thinking he'd won a mighty victory. When Jesus cried out to His Father, asking why He'd forsaken Him, the devil thought he'd succeeded in getting Him to question His Father's love. Then, when Jesus breathed His last and expired upon that cross, Satan did a victory dance, fully believing that his usual tactics had extinguished the voice of deliverance. "Another one bites the dust," he probably sang!

What Satan could not have foreseen is that though this cross killed the body of Christ, it didn't silence Him. In fact, the cross was part of God's plan from even before Creation to crush the head of Satan, overcome his works, and restore humanity back to the way God intended. As we'll explore more deeply in the coming chapters, the cross that was meant to silence Jesus was the instrument that actually silenced Satan.

The Cross Factor

Judas wasn't the only apostle to betray Jesus. At the same Last Supper where He foretold His betrayal by Judas, Jesus informed all the apostles that they too would give Him up. "You will all become deserters," He forewarned (Matt. 26:31). Peter couldn't conceive of such a notion and vowed he'd never do such a thing (v. 33). But talk is cheap. At the moment of Jesus's arrest in the Garden of Gethsemane, the Bible records that these so-called followers—Christ's closest companions—deserted Him, just as Jesus foretold. And Peter, the one who pledged liked Judas, "Surely not I," most surely did. When accused of being a follower of Christ, Peter vowed three times, "I do not know *the man*" (Matt. 26:70–74, emphasis added).

In the end each disciple betrayed Jesus—one for money, the others for the sake of their reputations. I'm sure each dealt with the accusations of Satan in their own ways. Peter, for example, wept bitterly (Luke 22:62). Still, they didn't share in

Judas's outcome. Peter went on to preach a sermon that converted more than three thousand people (Acts 2:41). Others, like Thomas, set out to evangelize and build churches in foreign lands.

You might suggest that the difference in outcomes has to do with the difference in the sin. Giving up Jesus for arrest is likely more tormenting than running away or claiming not to know Him, you might be thinking. But I think there's something deeper. I believe the difference is the cross.

Judas stopped short of the cross. He never had the chance to behold the suffering of Christ, or to see the greater resurrection plan in Christ's death. The others, however, intimately beheld His wounds. After His resurrection Jesus appeared to His disciples and showed them His visible marks of crucifixion (John 20:20, 27).

The cross has a healing power unlike anything else. There's something about beholding what Jesus did for you that's like a healing salve to wounds and a comfort for grief. This is what the prophets foretold: "By His bruises we are healed" (Isa. 53:5). This is what the other apostles experienced that Judas didn't.

Perhaps it's a mystery to you how an instrument of the greatest cruelty could be the means of restoration. But God's plan from the beginning was that Christ's cross gives way to resurrection life, free of the past and full of hope. We'll look much more closely at this in the next chapter.

The Crossroads

During the course of my attack I began to recognize Satan's plan in action. He wanted nothing more than to lead me down the road of Judas, to hang me by the same rope by which I was bound. Sure, he couldn't kill my flesh, nor could he steal my eternal destiny. My salvation was secure. But he could kill my voice and steal my potential. The accusations, anxiety, and evil forebodings were all part of his relentless scheme to silence me.

With this insight a revelation from God dropped into my spirit. I can still hear it so clearly. The Lord said, "You stand at a crossroads. You can take the road to the noose or to the nails. You can go to be hanged or to be held. But either way you will die." Those were my only two choices: the road of Judas or the road of Jesus. One would lead to the death of my voice, ministry, and destiny, which was Satan's goal. The other road would lead to the death of my flesh, but only so that God's plan of a resurrected life above the influences of Satan would be realized.

When I preach this message, I illustrate Satan's plan by tying a rope around me. The rope, of course, represents sin and the ways that Satan binds us. I then show how Satan holds this rope to drag us down his road of destruction, only to hang us with his lies, guilt, and shame at the end. I stand between two intersecting road signs. One reads, "Akeldama," the Field of Blood, where Judas was hanged. The other reads, "Via Dolorosa," the Way of the Cross, where Jesus was held. This "crossroads" is the visual representation of the dueling plans for your life.

Perhaps you too stand at this crossroads. Satan's temptations and whispers are unrelenting, and you're just about ready to give it all up. Or maybe you're already down the road to the noose. Satan has made you feel so dirty and worthless that you've given up any hope that God will use you. Wherever you stand right now, it's not too late to turn the tables on the devil and get on God's path to the place that ultimately silences Satan.

Throughout the next several chapters we'll travel the Way of the Cross. Like the apostles, we'll intimately look upon the punishment Jesus took so that we don't have to live with evil forebodings or fear God's wrath upon ourselves. We'll hear how His blood silences Satan by speaking in our defense. We'll understand just how Jesus dethroned the devil's dominion. And finally we'll learn how to die to all of those things that hold us back from this abundant, resurrected life that Jesus died to give.

Chapter 5

BEHOLD THE LAMB

WITH A SINGLE BITE OF THE BAIT OF SATAN, Adam and Eve quivered amongst the trees of the garden, naked and ashamed. How pitiful. Guilt led the crown of creation to hide amongst the very brush over which they were given dominion. With such a sense of worthlessness they simply couldn't bear to face the Creator.

We can be sure God wasn't pacing around heaven that day, worrying, "What do I do? What do I do?" This day was inevitable, and our all-knowing Father was prepared to put His plan in place. So despite their rebellion, God came down to initiate reconciliation with the first couple. He searched for Adam and Eve, hidden in the garden, to provide for them a covering so that they may live.

Throughout history God is always the initiator of reconciliation. The Bible details His relentless pursuits of people who went astray but meant so much to Him that He saved them. When the earth was dark and corrupt, the Lord pursued Noah to provide for him a way out of destruction. God called Abraham away from the life he'd known in order to build a family to bring blessing to the entire earth. To lengths as great as speaking through a burning bush, God appeared to Moses to lead His people out of their misery. In each case it was God who came looking.

God still relentlessly pursues us. He's not surprised or shaken by our shortcomings. When you succumb to temptation or feel beyond the point of no return, He doesn't say, "You're too far gone; I have to move on." No, He goes to great lengths to reveal to you the plan He put in place in order to bring you back to *life*. God is committed to relationship with you, and like any good father He wants to see you succeed.

In the moment of my despair God was faithful to show me His plan. He wouldn't let Satan's whispers succeed in taking me down the road to my doom. So He came looking for me— not through a burning bush or clouds of thunder, but rather God spoke to me through the still, small voice of Scripture. Within a resource I used to prepare for a television program, He brought my attention to the words of John the Baptist.

> Behold, the Lamb of God, who takes away the sin of the world!
> —JOHN 1:29, ESV

Initially, nothing about what John said really took me by surprise. I'd seen the verse countless times before, so I almost skipped over it out of sheer familiarity. But I was suddenly directed to just the single word, *behold*.

"Behold?" I wondered. "What could be so significant about that?"

It always astonishes me how I can read a verse of Scripture my entire life, but in just the right moment it's like God removes scales from my eyes and opens my understanding to something I've never seen before, something that changes everything. This was that kind of a profound moment.

I saw the weight of "behold" in its meaning.

behold—see or observe (a thing or a person, especially a remarkable or impressive one)[1]

Behold isn't a quick glance, but a close study. In this single verse John the Baptist directs us to see, observe, consider, look closely at, meditate, and fix our gaze upon the remarkable sight of Jesus as God's lamb, taking away the sin and shame of the world.

I came to learn I wasn't the only one who has received a similar revelation of these words. In fact, they've been esteemed and trumpeted by some of the great preachers of our time. British author and pastor Charles Spurgeon, known by many as the "Prince of Preachers," often spoke at length regarding John's words. In fact, Spurgeon believed this single announcement was the greatest sermon ever preached. "Nobody needs a new sermon when, 'Behold the Lamb of God,' is the old one," he said.[2]

Worthy Is the Lamb!

"Why is it that we must behold Jesus as a lamb?" some ask. It's a reasonable question, because, after all, the Bible describes Him in more than one hundred fifty ways. Why not fix our eyes upon Jesus as the kingly lion, protective and brave, who ravages His enemies; or the Bridegroom, compassionate and tender, patiently awaiting His eternal love?

Certainly those are endearing characteristics to ponder, but they aren't what the Bible considers the chief representation of Christ. In fact, there's no symbol used more throughout Scripture to describe Him than that of a lamb. The Book of Revelation alone refers to Him as a Lamb more than twenty-five times. It's what Jesus was ordained as from before the creation of the world (Rev. 13:8, KJV). "Like a lamb that is led to the slaughter" is the description given to us by the prophets

(Isa. 53:7). We'll see why in the next chapter, but the slain lamb is the sole image of reconciliation and acceptance with God.

Notice this: The elders seated around the emerald throne of God don't worship Jesus as worthy because of His great miracles, as awesome as they were. Nor do they cast down their crowns because of His teachings, so insightful and profound. Day and night the heavenly hosts fall before Jesus and cry, "Worthy is the *Lamb* that was slaughtered" (Rev. 5:12, emphasis added). Listen! Hear their worship to Jesus the Lamb.

> You are worthy to take the scroll and break its seals and open it. For you were slaughtered, and your blood has ransomed people for God from every tribe and language and people and nation. And you have caused them to become a Kingdom of priests for our God. And they will reign on the earth.
> —REVELATION 5:9–10, NLT

What a song! It's incredible. They sing of a ransom—the payment for the release of prisoners, the means of setting the captives free. The shed blood of the Lamb of God made the payment that provides the rescue of you and me from the clutches of Satan. And all the more, it establishes us as priests before God. We are men and women accepted by God, worthy to enter His presence, and approved for His service.

In this very moment those seated around heaven's crystal sea profess that Jesus is worthy because He became the promised Lamb that was slain. We too are made worthy by His blood, by which we share in His royal office on earth, have dominion over powers of darkness, and prop our feet upon the head of the devil.

Beyond the Cross

"See Calvary!" John the Baptist proclaimed. It's a call to go more intimately to the cross than ever before. Here we meet the One pierced for us. In this place, like Thomas, we examine His wounds. When we behold Jesus as the Lamb, we put ourselves at the foot of the cross and experience what Isaiah meant when he said, "By his bruises we are healed" (Isa. 53:5). The victory of the cross is made manifest in our lives when we get beyond just knowing about it and actually go to it ourselves.

Admittedly, in all of my Christian years, I'd never taken traveling the way of the cross as personally as I do now. From an early age I understood that Jesus died for my sins. In fact, I was raised in a church with a giant crucifix that hovered over and glared down from the front wall. Though I considered myself to have a close walk with Him, perhaps like Judas and Peter, out of sheer familiarity I let Jesus become just a mere *man* to me. And truthfully, through my time in seminary and professional ministry, I knew all there was to know about the cross and was beyond it—or so I thought.

Beyond the cross is a dangerous place to be, and that's precisely what gave the devil access to torment me in this moment. An animal that steps out of the covering of its habitat and into an open field is no longer hidden, but it is visible to every predator that hunts and seeks to devour it. The cross is our habitat. It's the place where Jesus instructed that our lives are to be lived daily (Luke 9:23). And when we stray from here, even for a moment, we step beyond God's protective covering and become an open target for the fiery arrows of the enemy.

With John's charge to "Behold the Lamb," I finally understood what the Lord meant when He offered me the choice to go to the nails. I knew that, painful as it may be, I needed to gaze into His suffering to encounter the weight of the stripes that crushed my habits and healed the pains of my past. "Look and live!" Charles Spurgeon said.[3] And that's what I did. With my mind's eye, there I went, to behold the Lamb of God.

Look and Live!

I invite you now to take your eyes off everything else and behold this Lamb. Put down your smartphone. Step away from the computer. Clear your mind of tomorrow's worries, and come with me to a hill outside of Jerusalem's city walls. Here an innocent man is suspended on a tree between two criminals. Focus your eyes only on Him. Hanging there merely by nails that pierced through His hands and His feet, He knows what your pain feels like. There He dangles on the world's stage, naked before creation; He understands your embarrassment and rejection. This man, tempted and tried in every way, can sympathize with your weaknesses (Heb. 4:15).

Behold this sight and witness no greater love. Peer in closely and grasp your hope. Hanging there is the man who bought your future. *He is* God's wonderful plan for your life. He is heaven's very best, dying so selflessly to give you a life of meaning and purpose.

Take it all in until you feel vulnerable again and your calloused heart softens. Gape deeper into His wounds; this is where your healing happens. See that your past and its wrongs are but a speck compared to the magnitude of the arms of grace stretched out across this rugged, splintery beam. Encounter Jesus until the grips by which you were bound now loosen. The wounds and burdens you've carried for what seems so long begin to dissolve. Here, fullness replaces emptiness. Passion supersedes numbness. Joy is traded for sorrow.

Inch your way to the foot of the cross, and let the wonder of Calvary envelop your senses. Take a deep breath of the sultry air; taste its bitterness. Look up at your Savior and allow that bottled-up grief to spring forth. It's OK to cry. It was prophesied that you would: "When they look on the one whom they have pierced, they shall mourn for him, as one mourns for an only child, and weep bitterly over him, as one weeps over a firstborn" (Zech. 12:10).

Focus upon the face of Jesus, spat on by the soldiers. His eyes are bloodshot from sleeplessness. A garland of twisted-together thorns atop His head serves as a mockery to this King of kings. With each jolt its one-inch barbs dig deeper and deeper into His maimed forehead. Scarlet streams race down His brow and mix with the tears of a broken heart. It's painful to see, I know, but His pain will heal yours.

Behold the Lamb of God, the final, once-for-all sacrifice, shredded upon the altar of the earth. An ocean of wrath consumes Him as wave upon wave of the punishment you and I deserved tortures His sinless body. Every lash from the Roman scourge leaves Him with chunks of flesh torn from His arms, chest, back, and legs. Its leather throngs knotted together with shrapnel continue to rip arteries, tendons, and nerves. Like flesh through the blades of a plow, there's your Deliverer, filleted from top to bottom.

It's a massacre unlike any other in history. Not an inch of His body is untouched by the cruelty. Deep lacerations, torn flesh, exposed bone, and wells of blood cover any human semblance; He's marred beyond recognition (Isa. 52:14).

Stop and pause here. Don't allow this moment to be fleeting. If you've just merely read through this, close your eyes and actually go there. *Behold the Lamb of God until you really see Him!* When you do, I promise, you'll experience the healing His wounds were meant to bring. After envisioning the cross in this way, people have reported physical healing to me. They've shared of broken addictions. One lady wrote, "I admit that I'd gotten stale, but I awoke with a new song and have a greater desire for boldness." Yes! These are the things that Jesus died to give you!

Hear His Words

The crowd around the cross is unruly. Mockers shout hateful slurs and scoff: "He saved others; let him save himself" (Luke 23:35). "Yeah!" another taunts. "If you are the king of the Jews, save yourself!" (v. 37). Soldiers laugh and carry on as they barter for the robes of this King.

If you're close enough, you hear wails from His women followers, beating their chests and wondering what went wrong. But tune out all of those voices and laser in on Jesus. Listen! Hear the words of the pierced One transcending time to speak to you today.

"Father, forgive them."

The thieves to His right and His left aren't the only criminals who surround Him. The hateful mockers, the cruel soldiers, the greedy Judas, the cowered disciples, and the masses who yelled, "Crucify Him"—they all played a part in this day.

But the sins that now consume Jesus aren't theirs alone. Those sins are also yours and mine. His wounds represent the past, present, and future mistakes of the entire world. We're the thieves who stole His innocence and put our filth upon Him. We're the criminals who ought to be on that middle tree, but instead there's Jesus, serving our death sentence for us.

This is yet another moment in history when God could have given up on the human race, scrapped it all, and started over. But He doesn't relent. Instead He cries out from His tree of execution:

> Father, forgive them; for they do not know what they
> are doing.
> —LUKE 23:34

My eyes glaze with tears when I behold the enormity of what Jesus said. "Father, forgive Kyle, for he didn't/doesn't know what he did/is doing/will do." Replace my name with yours, and hear Him cry out for you too.

It's true; we didn't know what we were doing and we don't know what we'll do in the future. As we've already said, we rarely see sin's consequences played out in the moment of temptation. But Jesus's words divert the wrath of God and silence the accusations of Satan against us. If you ever wanted a definition of grace, this is it: "Father, don't hold their ignorance against them; don't punish them for their guilt," Jesus cries. "I take it all upon Me in order that they may live!"

"Here is your son; here is your mother."

Now you must draw in closer because an intimate moment is about to happen. The most loyal followers of Jesus are always the ones closest to the cross. And so, nearly hugging that tree are Jesus's mother, Mary; her sister; Mary Magdalene; and John, the disciple whom Jesus loved (John 19:25).

John is the disciple who remained the closest to Jesus. He leaned on Jesus's chest at the Last Supper (John 13:23) and is the only one of the twelve that the Bible mentions was present, at least this closely, at the cross. The events of the day must have been monumental for him; the cross always leaves a lasting impact on those who have beheld it. To John, Jesus wasn't just a mere man; He was his Lord, the Lamb of God that he personally witnessed taking away the sins of the world. It's not surprising, then, that John is the author of Revelation, in which he describes the heavenly Lamb so many times.

When Jesus takes His eyes off the crowd for whom He'd just

asked for forgiveness, He looks down and sees His mother and John stricken with grief. Filled with compassion, Jesus speaks:

> "Woman, here is your son." Then he said to the disciple, "Here is your mother."
> —JOHN 19:26–27

At the foot of the cross Jesus creates a family. He entrusts His mother to the care of His beloved disciple, John; He entrusts John to the care of His mother. They're bonded together at the cross, where they're cared for from that day forward.

I take Christ's words to Mary and John for myself. When I began my born-again relationship with Jesus, I did so without the approval of my family. For many years I was the son who bucked the ol' family tradition, and I suffered much pain from being rejected and misunderstood by those closest to me. I'm thankful that, in God's timing, He turned this around. But for years I clung to the reality of the what the psalmist wrote: "If my father and mother forsake me, the LORD will take me up" (Ps. 27:10).

Whatever your situation, Jesus speaks to you too. If you're rejected by those closest to you, God comforts, "I chose you!" If you're orphaned and have never known the love of a family, God says, "Welcome to Mine!" If you're the victim of abuse or an absent father, God assures, "I'm your loving Father." If you don't feel good enough to be part of God's family, He declares, "You're forgiven!" There's a bond made in the intimacy of the cross that adopts you into a family where you'll never be abandoned (Heb. 13:5).

"Why have You forsaken Me?"

Suddenly the sky turns dark, and for the next three hours thick, ferocious thunderheads billow one on top of the other. Something big is about to happen; don't miss it! The thrashings pause as Jesus adds His own roar to the rumblings of the impending storm. Hear Him thunder:

> "Eli, Eli, lema sabachthani?" that is, "My God, my God, why have you forsaken me?"
> —MATTHEW 27:46

This is the most heart-wrenching cry ever heard upon this earth! It's God crying out to God, but not to complain of the pain. He doesn't cry, "Father, why did You allow this crown of thorns upon My head?" or "Why must My hands and feet be pierced with nails?" Christ's deepest anguish isn't the scourge or the spears; it's the rejection of His Father.

In this moment a transformation is finished. Jesus is completely in the form of sin; He's now entirely in our place. This is the event ordained from the beginning of time. Jesus is so saturated with the guilt of the world that the Father has to hide His eyes and break relationship with His Son, even if just for a moment.

The revelation that Jesus took humankind's place upon the cross is ultimately what led Martin Luther into his reformation. Luther used to beat himself as a way to "pay" for his sins. He wrestled with Jesus's cry, asking, "Why would God forsake His own Son?" But in the height of his grappling, he found the answer to the mystery: *If Christ took on the sins of the world, then that includes my sins too. This means I no longer carry the guilt of my sin, and need not punish myself.*[4]

We can all relate to Luther in some way. Perhaps you don't flog yourself, but do you often pay for your sin with days or weeks of guilt, a sulking attitude, or a negative opinion of yourself? I used to think I had to pay for it with silence. When I'd mess up, I'd figure, "I better not speak up in the Bible study this week. I'm not good enough to post a Facebook status today." This is exactly the goal of Satan's accusations. He wants you to beat yourself up—to try and pay a fine that has already been paid. *But Jesus was forsaken by God so that you and I are never forsaken by God.* Now there's no condemnation or punishment to be had. You're free to enjoy a guilt-free life on God's side!

The Greatest Pursuit

Jesus thunders one final roar to ultimately silence and mark the end of Satan's reign forever. We'll hear and explore the declaration that defeated the devil in chapter 6. But now He bows His head and breathes His last. Expired upon that tree is a man who knew no sin but became sin *for you* (2 Cor. 5:21). This perfect man took on the filth, the shame, and all its consequences for the very people who murdered Him. Think about it! He was born to suffer and die a brutal death for things He wasn't guilty of, so that you and I may be forgiven, included in the Father's family, and avert punishment. He did it all so that we may have eternal, resurrected life with Him.

> For God so loved the world that he gave his only Son, so that everyone who believes in him may not perish but may have eternal life.
>
> —JOHN 3:16

Behold this fathomless love! Out of this love God emptied Himself of His godliness and took on the form of a human. In human form He selflessly fulfilled His mission to die (Phil. 2:7–8).

Compelled by love, the cross was God's greatest pursuit of you. He left the brilliance of heaven to identify with your pain so that He could lead you out of it and show you the better way. He hung upon that tree of scorn to demonstrate to you that He knows the sting of rejection and humiliation. He understands what it's like to feel worthless. He felt the breath of Satan upon His face and the pressure of every temptation. *Jesus understands you.* He chased you from heaven to prove that these things don't have to define you; they don't have to defeat you. The life He lived and the death He died show that sin and its consequences may be victoriously overcome.

When I decided to travel the way of the cross, I finally beheld Jesus like never before. Those words of John the Baptist awakened me to the crux of the faith—the centerpiece of salvation that I had unfortunately forgotten. With this intimate beholding, my mind was so consumed with Calvary's love and a love for Calvary that I fell to my knees, and on many occasions thereafter all I could do was cry.

I found a life that day unlike anything I'd known before—no longer a partly transformed life with a Christian label, but the abundant, resurrected, new life that Jesus promised. The wounds of Jesus healed and emboldened me, and I found the place of victory that I longed for. It was always there at the cross, but I had to go there to experience it—to *behold* it—for myself. When I did, I resolved to live in this place for the rest of my life.

Chapter 6

THE BLOOD THAT SPEAKS

WHEN MEL GIBSON'S *THE PASSION OF THE CHRIST* was released, considerable controversy surrounded the gruesomeness of the film. The media viciously attacked why it pictured Jesus so ripped to shreds. One commentator wrote: "*The Passion of the Christ* is messy. From Jesus' violent arrest to his flogging and crucifixion, almost every scene is marked by callous cruelty and bloodshed. Jesus' bruised right eye swells shut. Deep lacerations crisscross his flesh."[1]

The journalist didn't understand the film's obsession with blood. "How much blood and violence are necessary, I found myself wondering, for the crucifixion story to be authentic?"[2]

The movie is a masterpiece and, arguably, the best cinematic portrayal of Christ's crucifixion to date. In fact, when I preach the message of the last chapter, about beholding Jesus as the Lamb that was slain, I often display a screenshot from *The Passion of the Christ*. Still, the answer to the reporter's question? More! In fact, it's not that *The Passion of the Christ* contains too much blood, but rather, not enough blood.

Foretelling of Christ's crucifixion, the prophet Isaiah wrote:

But many were amazed when they saw him. His face
was so disfigured he seemed hardly human, and from
his appearance, one would scarcely know he was a man.

—ISAIAH 52:14, NLT

Though *The Passion of the Christ* is certainly one of the
bloodiest depictions on film, it doesn't completely fit the Bible's
description of the authentic crucifixion, because in the movie
Christ is still recognizable as a man. To think that less blood
is necessary is to grossly misunderstand the gospel and how
much it hinges upon Christ's excruciatingly bloody sacrifice.

Offended by the Blood?

At one time Christianity was proud of the blood. It was
known for its songs that boasted in Christ's DNA. Maybe
you've heard these hopeful lyrics: "What can wash away my
sin? Nothing but the blood of Jesus. What can make me whole
again? Nothing but the blood of Jesus."[3] Or these lively lines:
"There is power, power, wonder-working power in the blood of
the Lamb!"[4] For years the church knew that its lifeblood—its
very essence, strength, and vitality—was in the blood of Jesus.
The blood was esteemed as the source of salvation, deliverance,
healing, and life itself.

The church today has plenty of self-help and life enhance-
ment messages, but lately I've noticed very little teaching
about the blood of Jesus, almost as if it's been drained from
the modern gospel. Rather than boasting in the blood, some
are downright offended by it. I've heard parents complain
when their elementary-aged children are taught about Christ's
crucifixion—in a Christian school. "It might cause nightmares,"
they protest. A popular Christian personality even suggests
that the blood of Jesus is no longer relevant to people today.

There's nothing wrong with talking and singing about how the "Blood will never lose its power" and "Nothing but the blood will save us." Those are powerful metaphors. But we don't live any longer in a culture in which people offer animal sacrifices to the gods. People did live that way for thousands of years, and there are pockets of primitive cultures around the world that do continue to understand sin, guilt, and atonement in those ways. But most of us don't. What the first Christians did was look around them and put the Jesus story in language their listeners would understand.[5]

The author's suggestion that most people today don't understand sin, guilt, and atonement in those ways is itself out of touch. The word *atonement* contains three parts combined: at-one-ment. It actually means "at one with God," which is the state of being in relationship with God. Many people today have an overwhelming sense that *something* is wrong with them, even if they don't completely know what it is. They walk laden with guilt, shame, and condemnation. And so their prevailing question is, "Why is God so mad at me?" They'd love to be "at one" with their Creator, but they've succumbed to the lies and accusations of Satan that they can't be in relationship with God because of their sin and guilt.

Many have tried to find reconciliation with God in all of the wrongs ways and have given up hope of ever finding it. They don't understand that the key to relationship with God is found in the blood of Jesus only because they haven't been taught, not because the blood is irrelevant.

The fact is, people today struggle intensely as Satan launches his rigorous campaign against a generation. Spiritual warfare is at its height, and the Bible says that our only hope to overcome Satan's schemes is the blood of Jesus. What could be more relevant?

> But they have conquered him by the blood of the
> Lamb and by the word of their testimony, for they did
> not cling to life even in the face of death.
>
> —REVELATION 12:11

To conquer something is to overtake it, rise above it, and take authority over it. If you want to live free from temptation, above the voice of Satan, and with the resurrected life that Jesus died to give, the blood of Jesus is the only source for your power! It's the highest octane of gasoline in your engine to resist the devil. Satan knows that the blood is the key to his defeat, which is why he works so craftily to remove it from the only place where it may be found—the church.

Why Blood?

Like it or not, the Bible is a bloody book. From beginning to end it revels in blood. But why? Why is God so obsessed with gore? First, you must understand, to God, blood isn't gore. Sin is what has made it gory. When you see disease and sickness, you might see blood. When you hear of a murder, often you picture a tragic blood slaughter. Where there's a car accident, there's almost always great bloodshed. And so we view blood as the most disgusting representation of everything that's wrong with the world. None of these are God's original design, but the results of sin. Sin is what perverted blood and equated it with death. God, however, created blood to represent life.

> For the life of the flesh is in the blood.
>
> —LEVITICUS 17:11

More than anything else in the body, blood is essential to life. It's what carries the fuel and oxygen to the billions of cells in our bodies. Blood supplies the brain and the heart with the necessary nourishment to function. It also carries carbon dioxide and other waste materials to the digestive system, where they are then removed from the body. Without blood we couldn't keep warm or cool, fight infections, or get rid of our own waste products.[6] Additionally, our very identity—our DNA—is located in our blood. God is so obsessed with blood because He's so obsessed with life.

Blood in the Garden

While science knows a great deal about why blood is so vital to life, there's much it doesn't know about the importance that God places on it. The first indication of blood in the Bible has to do with covering Adam and Eve's guilt and shame, and replacing their death with life.

After the first couple gave in to the temptations of the sinister serpent and immediately realized their nakedness, they attempted to cover themselves with fig leaves and loincloths (Gen. 3:7). I believe they did their best to try and make themselves presentable to God for when He'd find them hiding amongst the trees of the garden. This is a perfect example of religion—our attempts to be presentable to God. We craft so many rules, programs, and doctrines that try to impress God or gain His favor. But in the end our ways just aren't good enough. Our relationship with God is restored based on His free gift, not on anything we can concoct.

Adam and Eve's attempt to cover their sin and shame wasn't good enough. Fig leaves aren't alive—they're dead. Because of their sin Adam and Eve weren't alive either—they were dead. Life can't be restored with something that's dead. And so God had to give them a gift of His own—a covering of life. The Bible says, "The LORD God made garments of skins for the man and for his wife, and clothed them" (v. 21).

I truly believe that God chose some animals for a sacrifice and used the animals' skins, freshly wetted with blood, to cover Adam and Eve. God chose to cover their sin and shame with blood—with life!

Like Adam and Eve, we are just as aware of our need of a covering. We attempt to handle our guilt and shame in all the wrong ways too. Previously I mentioned how I tried to hide my shame with things like overachieving, perfectionism, and keeping distant relationships. Others cope through addictions, medications, alcohol, unhealthy relationships, and lifestyles of sin. Everyone is looking for ways to manage their struggles, which is why, contrary to the opinion of some in the modern church, atonement is extremely relevant for today.

The Blood of Atonement

Untamed sin has a downward spiraling effect. It doesn't take long after sin is introduced into a situation for everything to get a bit crazy. Many of us know this all too well. One quick peak at a sensual image becomes wasted hours and days pursuing the lusts of the flesh. A seemingly innocent conversation with another man's wife turns into endless text messages, phone calls, and nights of regret. A dabble with a drink becomes a constant coping method by which, day after day, you cast your cares upon the bottle. This all began after Adam and Eve's fall when humanity went into a state of upheaval and sin and death took over (Rom. 5:14). God's solution to this crazy sin cycle was to institute animal blood sacrifices.

> Indeed, under the law almost everything is purified with blood, and without the shedding of blood there is no forgiveness of sins.
> —HEBREWS 9:22

Again, God's requirement for sacrifices isn't because He's cruel and bloodthirsty, but because He loves life. Sin is equated with death (Gen. 2:17; Rom. 6:23), and death can only be reversed with life. Knowing this, let's replace the word *blood* with *life* and the word *sin* with *death* in the scripture above. Here's how it reads: "Everything is purified with life, and without life there is no forgiveness of death."

Humanity's sin separated them from their Creator. People could no longer enjoy the same relationship that Adam and Eve once experienced with God. Sin is the great firewall, and nothing of God can penetrate a life when it's covered with sin. Because of this, God instituted His sacrificial system to restore humanity's broken relationship with Him.

> For the life of the flesh is in the blood; and I have given it to you for making atonement for your lives on the altar; for, as life, it is the blood that makes atonement.
> —LEVITICUS 17:11

Blood dissolves the firewall between humanity and God so that it can again be "at one" with Him. This is the covenant the Lord made with His people. In order to stay in relationship with God, a high priest had to repeat this act on behalf of the people once a year on a day known as the "Day of Atonement." And for thousands of years the people of God went through the lengths of offering the blood of untainted goats and lambs so that they could be made right with their Creator.

The Final Lamb

Revelation refers to Jesus as "the Lamb slain from the foundation of the world" (Rev. 13:8, KJV). This is incredible! What this says is that, from the creation of the world, God had a plan to resurrect humankind from its death. He made a covenant with Himself that when everything went awry, He would personally become the blood sacrifice necessary to bring you and me back into relationship with Him. From the very first sacrifice in the Garden of Eden through the yearly sacrifices by the high priests of Israel, God prepared the world for the arrival of the One who would become the final, once-for-all sacrifice.

Jesus is that sacrifice. He's called a lamb because He represents the lamb of the Old Testament sacrifices. The lamb or goat had to be spotless and without blemish. Jesus lived such a life—perfect and free of defect; His blood was uncorrupted by sin.

> Knowing that you were not redeemed with corruptible things, like silver or gold…but with the precious blood of Christ, as of a lamb without blemish and without spot.
> —1 PETER 1:18–19, NKJV

Notice that this scripture equates corruptible things with silver, gold, and anything less than Christ's blood. If you're trying to "work off" your past sins or pay a penance for your guilt and shame through your church service or charitable deeds, you'll only wear yourself out. Even if you help one thousand old ladies across the street within the next week, your good-hearted acts can't redeem you. Money, possessions, and a lavish lifestyle won't satisfy either. Hear Scripture loud and clear: the blood of Jesus is your *only* solution for a bold, resurrected life in good standing with God and to be made worthy of every blessing that He has to offer.

What we beheld in the last chapter—the body of Jesus mutilated, ripped to shreds, and drenched in blood—was Jesus undergoing the final sacrifice that would end our guilt and shame. He endured every thorn, lash, and nail to put us back into permanent relationship with God. In His final minutes hanging upon the cross, Jesus cried out, "It is finished." In the next chapter we'll explore what Jesus meant by this, but after these last words, He bowed His head and gave up His spirit (John 19:30).

Covered With Life

In the first chapter we established that Jesus came to give us abundant life (John 10:10). We saw that this life, which is the Greek word *zoe*, is a resurrected life. It's not a life haunted by the past, but made new and made right, as if the past never happened. This is the sole purpose that Jesus laid down His life in such a bloody way (v. 11).

Paul instructs us to "put on the Lord Jesus Christ" (Rom. 13:14). To put on Jesus is to be clothed in a covering of abundant life. Life, as we know, is active and full of energy; it breathes and speaks. When you're covered with Jesus, you're covered with His blood, which constantly works to restore what was once dead and to ward off Satan by speaking on your behalf.

> ...Jesus, the mediator of a new covenant, and to the sprinkled blood that speaks a better word than the blood of Abel.
> —HEBREWS 12:24

Abel's blood cries out for revenge (Gen. 4:10), but Jesus's blood cries out, "Forgiven!" The blood is like a force field that surrounds and protects you. I'm convinced that some Christians live defeated lives because they either don't know or are too lazy to put on Christ! Make it a practice to wake up in the morning and declare aloud, "I put on Christ and cover myself in His blood." Christ's blood covering is the greatest weapon against the devil because it counters his lies and shouts back at him in your defense. Here are three powerful defenses the blood of Jesus makes on your behalf.

"Move on!"

At the time when Israel was about to be led out of Egypt's grip, God instituted a "Passover" to aid their escape. The night before their exodus the Lord commanded the families of Israel to make a blood sacrifice from a spotless lamb and then coat their doorposts with this blood.

> They shall take some of the blood and put it on the two doorposts and the lintel of the houses in which they eat it.... For I will pass through the land of Egypt that night, and I will strike down every firstborn in the land of Egypt, both human beings and animals; on all the gods of Egypt I will execute judgments: I am the LORD. The blood shall be a sign for you on the houses where you live: when I see the blood, I will pass over you, and no plague shall destroy you when I strike the land of Egypt.
>
> —EXODUS 12:7, 12–13

Israel was ultimately delivered from their slavery in Egypt because the blood of a pure, spotless lamb identified them as God's people, and therefore they couldn't be touched by death.

Covered in Jesus's blood, you too are identified as a child of God. When the devourer comes to tempt, accuse, or destroy you, he sees the blood and hears, "They have conquered him by the blood of the Lamb" (Rev. 12:11). With this he must move on!

"Worthy!"

When you are covered in the blood of Jesus, God sees you through a bloodstained lens. That is, when He looks at you, He no longer sees sin and shame, but He sees the pure, spotless life of His Son, Jesus. The sole reason why God declares you righteous and worthy isn't because of anything you've done, but because His Son is righteous and worthy. As we saw with Adam and Eve, human efforts are futile, but God's gift of Jesus's blood restores us back to good standing with Him.

> In him we have redemption through his blood, the forgiveness of our trespasses, according to the riches of his grace that he lavished on us.
> —EPHESIANS 1:7–8

When Satan barges into the throne room of heaven to plead his accusations against you to God, the Lord sends him away with a poignant reminder of the blood of Jesus. When he comes down to whisper his accusations in your ear, the blood silences him, retorting, "There is therefore now no condemnation for those who are in Christ Jesus" (Rom. 8:1).

"Accepted!"

According to the Old Testament's sacrificial system, only the high priest could enter the Most Holy Place where the presence of the Lord lived.

> But only the high priest ever entered the Most Holy Place, and only once a year. And he always offered blood for his own sins and for the sins the people had committed in ignorance.
> —HEBREWS 9:7, NLT

Only once per year could the high priest enter God's presence, and he didn't dare do so without an offering of blood. The blood covering is what made the priest acceptable and able to stand in God's sight.

The blood of Jesus gives you and me constant access to God's presence without fear of rejection. Even better, the blood allows us to *boldly* enter God's presence.

> Let us therefore approach the throne of grace with
> boldness, so that we may receive mercy and find grace
> to help in time of need.
>
> —HEBREWS 4:16

You no longer need to fear that God is mad at you and ready to zap you dead at any moment. God accepts you into His presence and offers you an intimate relationship to talk to Him about anything, at any time. When the devil tries to convince you that God is distant, and therefore doesn't care about your everyday needs, the blood responds, "But now in Christ Jesus you who once were far off have been brought near by the blood of Christ" (Eph. 2:13).

The Benefits of the Blood

David boasted in the Lord and made it a point to always remember God's benefits.

> Bless the LORD, O my soul, and do not forget all his
> benefits—who forgives all your iniquity, who heals all
> your diseases, who redeems your life from the Pit.
>
> —PSALM 103:2–4

I believe that the church should return to boasting in the blood! I never fail to walk in greater levels of victory against sin and guilt when I'm sure to consider the blood and its benefits on a daily basis. I promise that you too will live in greater victory if you make it a point each day to cover yourself in Christ and His blood.

Let's recap the blood's benefits:

◊ We receive forgiveness of sins (Matt. 26:28).

◊ We are made innocent and freed from guilt and
  shame (Rom. 5:9).

◊ We are declared worthy and righteous
  (2 Cor. 5:21).

◊ We can silence Satan's temptations and accusations (Rev. 12:11).

◊ We can have boldness to ask God for help
  (Heb. 4:16).

◊ We can enjoy daily relationship with God
  (Eph. 2:13).

These are but a few of the tremendous benefits given because of Christ's bloody sacrifice on the cross. With these, who would dare claim that the blood is irrelevant today? There's no forgiveness, healing, deliverance, or salvation without the blood of Jesus. Rather than question how little blood I can get by with, I'd rather stand under the cross to be covered in all that I can get!

Go again with your mind's eye to behold Jesus as the Lamb that was slain. Say aloud: "I cover myself in Your blood, Jesus." Now picture it envelop you from head to toe, not one part of you untouched by its deep scarlet. Hear it speak in your defense and deflect Satan's lies. If the devil taunts, "Bound!", the blood assures, "Free!" If the devil fires, "Rejected!", the blood responds, "Accepted!" If the devil threatens, "Sick!", the blood proclaims, "Healed!" If the devil accuses, "Guilty!", the blood declares, "Forgiven!" Yes! The blood of Jesus silences Satan!

Chapter 7

MARCHING 'EM NAKED

THE MORNING THAT I WENT SO PERSONALLY TO the cross and finally beheld Jesus as the lamb slain for my sins—when I sobbed for an hour, when I saw my sin as exceedingly sinful—I received a sudden prompting from the Spirit of God. It wasn't audible, but more like a gentle word dropped into my spirit that instructed, "Make a record of your wrongs." "A record of my wrongs?" I questioned. I wondered if this was just another whisper of the accuser trying to bring back to mind more of my regrets. But something about this voice was different; it was calm and assuring, not nagging and condemning.

Nervously I got up off the floor and scrambled around my room for a paper large enough to make this list. A piece of college-ruled loose leaf had to do. I nestled into my couch to begin this very painful process.

I didn't have to think too hard to list my sins; the devil kept them fresh on my mind for the last week. Still, I was tempted to jot down only generalities. But whom was I kidding? I sat there in that empty apartment, just God and me, and we both knew everything there was to know about me. So with nothing to hide and no façade to keep, I got very specific and—line by line—admitted my most secret and grievous sins to a confessional of paper. Some of these I had never dealt with, and some I apparently hadn't fully dealt with. By the end of that agonizing exercise I had a paper that looked like an indictment for arrest!

After this, something fresh dropped into my spirit. It was a familiar passage of Scripture from Colossians, but in light of the circumstances it took on a profoundly new meaning to me.

> When you were stuck in your old sin-dead life, you were incapable of responding to God. God brought you alive—right along with Christ! Think of it! All sins forgiven, the slate wiped clean, that old arrest warrant canceled and nailed to Christ's cross. He stripped all the spiritual tyrants in the universe of their sham authority at the Cross and marched them naked through the streets.
> —COLOSSIANS 2:13–15, THE MESSAGE

As I read this passage, I immediately recognized it as a description of me. I was stuck in a rut that was intended to lead to my destruction. The secret sins, guilt, and shame all kept me bound from an on-fire life for God. In fact, these were the source of Satan's authority in my life, which allowed him to keep reminding me of my crimes. His aim was to use this warrant for my execution—to be hanged—and to make me another casualty of his plan to steal and kill and destroy.

But God's plan relentlessly pursues us! In this moment I saw the key to finally silence Satan and live victoriously. It's the cross! By His grace He led me to the cross to personally witness the One wounded for me. Again I envisioned the nails, but this time piercing through every accusation and sin inked on that paper. It was just as the scripture read: "That old arrest warrant canceled and nailed to Christ's cross!"

For the first time in more than a week I felt victory arise in me. It had nothing to do with me or what little strength or accolades I possessed. Rather, it was the absolute assurance that the cross of Christ dethroned Satan in my life and set me at peace with God. My sorrow began to turn to joy, and for the next ten minutes I grabbed my pen to draw a cross and write "blood" on that paper. Over and over again I retraced a cross and wrote "blood" until that list of regrets was covered by representations of the only two things that can actually cover sin.

A song we loved to sing as young school-aged children in church is titled "No Fishing!" It's a catchy, simple ditty, but with lyrics much too profound for a first grader. This song simply stated that when Jesus forgives us, He forgets the things we did. In fact, what He does is actually throw the bad things we did into God's forgetful sea. And once He has done that, He places a huge sign there that reads: NO FISHING.

With the newfound revelation of my record of wrongs nailed to the cross, I knew I had to obliterate the list. So I ripped that paper to shreds and threw the remnants into that forgetful sea, never to be fished out again.

It Is Finished!

Now, as clearly as all the other whispers and voices, I heard a declaration: "It is finished!" I immediately recognized this steadfast statement as the final words of Christ just before He took His last breath.

> When Jesus had received the wine, he said, "It is finished." Then he bowed his head and gave up his spirit.
> —JOHN 19:30

"It is finished" is the translation of the Greek word *tetelestai*. According to documents found from New Testament times, this word was often written across the top of receipts or promissory notes to indicate a bill paid in full. Another example was from when a father sent his son out on a mission. The son was not to come back home until the mission was accomplished. Upon success of the mission, the son returned proclaiming, "*Tetelestai!*"[1]

I believe that Jesus cried out "It is finished!" with a bellow that all of creation could hear. "The bill is paid!" He exclaimed. "The mission is complete!" With Jesus's bloody crucifixion, the wages of death that sin was owed was paid once and for all. He had successfully completed what His Father sent Him to do. In that moment Satan and his minions must have begun to shake in their boots and wonder, "What does He mean by 'It is finished'?" They thought they'd silenced the voice of deliverance, but they didn't yet realize that in this moment it was their voices that were silenced. And this was the ultimate purpose of Christ's mission.

> The Son of God was revealed for this purpose, to destroy the works of the devil.
> —1 JOHN 3:8

Slavery to sin is finished.

As we've seen, from the moment Adam and Eve conceded to the deceit of Satan, their God-given authority was stolen; Satan became the god of this world, and creation was under his power (1 John 5:18). With this, the dominion of sin and death took over, enslaving humanity to its grip (Rom. 5:14).

Those habits and addictions that you just can't seem to break free from—the negative thoughts that bombard your mind, the persistent feeling of condemnation—these are the results of sin's enslavement. Perhaps you were lured in by the perception of freedom and life without rules. Sin probably felt good for a while and appeared pleasant. This is the bait that Eve bit into as well. But it attaches to you like a bungee cord. You won't feel its clutch until you go too far and it violently slings you back to where you started. Sin's attachment can't be cut on your own, which is why Christ went to the cross.

> Since therefore the children share in flesh and blood, he himself likewise partook of the same things, that through death he might destroy the one who has the power of death, that is, the devil, and deliver all those who through fear of death were subject to lifelong slavery.
> —HEBREWS 2:14–15, ESV

Jesus's death *destroyed* the one who seeks to kill and the power of his plan, which is slavery to sin. The nails of the cross hammered through sin's hold on you and severed its cord. With His last breath Jesus proclaimed release to the captives and freedom to the oppressed (Luke 4:18). The hill of Calvary exalted the true King of creation, and He has "set you free to live openly in his freedom" (Rom. 6:18, THE MESSAGE).

Condemnation is finished.

With sin's dominion comes condemnation, which is just another word for persistent guilt and shame. It's the constant feeling that God disapproves of you. We've seen how this affected Adam and Eve and caused them to craft their own coverings and hide from God. Sin and condemnation work in partnership with each other. Remember from chapter 1 how Satan sets us up: sin is the trap, and condemnation is the noose that hangs us.

As blood covered the shame of the first couple, Christ's

excruciatingly bloody sacrifice covered sin's shame for all time and set us free from ever having to feel disapproved of by God.

> There is therefore now no condemnation for those who are in Christ Jesus. For the law of the Spirit of life in Christ Jesus has set you free from the law of sin and death.
>
> —ROMANS 8:1–2

Freedom from the law of sin and death is freedom from condemnation. When Jesus declared, "It is finished," He put Satan on notice that the power of His accusations is canceled in heaven and on earth. That record of your wrongs that Satan uses to badger you has *tetelestai* stamped across it. The fine for your sin is paid in full by perfect blood; there's no need for guilt and shame. You can be confident that Satan's arrest warrant against you is canceled because the nails of the cross have pierced its power. The hauntings from your past are silenced, you're declared worthy, and you're now free to fulfill God's mission for your life!

Fear that God is mad is finished.

I remember a time when I was young that I stole a toy from a neighbor girl. I'm not sure how they realized the toy was missing, but as is usually the case, my sin found me out, and my neighbor's mom approached me to ask why I stole it. I recall feeling incredibly ashamed for my actions, and for the next couple weeks I did everything that I could to avoid her, simply because I perceived she was mad at me. I didn't need to tiptoe around her like that for so long. She had forgiven me, but my guilt kept me at a distance.

The power that sin and condemnation has in our lives is that it keeps us feeling that God is angry, and therefore we hold Him at a distance. But Jesus took God's anger upon Himself, and at the cross the wrath of God was satisfied. Now God's not mad at you; He's mad *about* you!

> But God proves his love for us in that while we still were sinners Christ died for us. Much more surely then, now that we have been justified by his blood, will we be saved through him from the wrath of God.
>
> —ROMANS 5:8–9

The great news is that the cross secures us in the love of God, which Satan has no power to separate (Rom. 8:39). And whatever is in love is in relationship. That intimate friendship that Adam and Eve enjoyed with God before their fall is now yours to enjoy. Look at the cross, and you'll see the answer to the question "Does God love me?" There's Jesus, arms stretched open wide, boasting, "I love you this big!"

The Ultimate Gotcha!

I often say that the devil is nearsighted. What I mean by this is that he frequently sees only what's so obviously in front of him, and, fortunately for us, he misses the larger plan. In that moment it looked like Satan had lured Jesus to His death and, thus, extinguished salvation. He knew the scripture that says, "Anyone hung on a tree is under God's curse" (Deut. 21:23), and he really believed that he had won the final victory, overcome the curse God placed upon him back in the garden, and killed the Son of God.

But Jesus was known for turning tables...

The plan from the beginning

The cross didn't take God by surprise; in fact, it was His plan all along. The Book of Revelation refers to Jesus as the

"Lamb slain from the foundation of the world" (Rev. 13:8, KJV). Peter said the same:

> You know that you were ransomed from the futile ways inherited from your ancestors, not with perishable things like silver or gold, but with the precious blood of Christ, like that of a lamb without defect or blemish. *He was destined before the foundation of the world, but was revealed at the end of the ages for your sake.*
> —1 PETER 1:18–20,
> emphasis added

What these verses say is that before the world was created, God made a covenant with Himself. Perhaps you might even call it an insurance policy. Because the policy was taken out and paid before the incident ever occurred, it covered everything fully and completely. No one knew about this plan, not even Satan, and it was all revealed in its glory on the cross.

Wounded for our transgressions

Sin simply means to "miss the mark" and is a general term for an act that's the opposite of doing right. Scripture breaks sin into at least two categories, "transgression" and "iniquity," and the differences between the two are significant.

A transgression is a presumptuous sin; it's the act of intentional disobedience. When you make the conscious choice to tell a lie, run the red light, or cheat on your test, you've just committed a transgression. An iniquity, on the other hand, is a premeditated choice that continues without repentance.[2] These are the potent sins that enslave us. Constant drunkenness, sexual immorality, or any habitual lifestyle is considered an iniquity. But God's plan for the cross was to obliterate the power of these snares!

> But he was wounded for our transgressions, crushed
> for our iniquities; upon him was the punishment that
> made us whole, and by his bruises we are healed.
>
> —ISAIAH 53:5

The punctures in Christ's hands and feet, the piercing in His side, and the flesh ripped from His bones—these were all endured to pay for our intentional acts of disobedience. The crown of thorns pierced His skull, the weight of sin crushed His body, and the grief of Calvary crushed His will. These all occurred so that the addictions, secret sins, and cycles of shame would be displaced. Satan didn't have a clue that the extreme punishment that mutilated the Son of God to the point that He no longer looked like a man was all along set up to destroy his evil works.

Death defeated

As we've seen, up until this point in history the law of sin and death reigned. No one had ever overcome what seemed to be inevitable—death always follows sin. So when Jesus hung from that cross, covered with the sins of the world, it appeared that God's mission had failed. He hadn't become the King the prophets expected, nor was He the political force the government feared.

It sure looked like the end for this man who in just three years of public ministry turned the world upside down. Even His women followers, who up until this point were some of His most optimistic supporters, gave up hope. After they witnessed His fight to take His last breath, the crowds returned home in deep sorrow (Luke 23:48). They prepared His burial in a tomb with plenty of spices according to the traditional Jewish embalming procedures (v. 56). What seemed to have such promise and a great destiny was beaten, battered, bruised beyond description, and laid in a tomb waiting to decay. What went wrong?

They should have known that it wasn't all over. But tragedy has a way of blinding people to hope. We become so focused on the pain that seems will never end, and suddenly we lose all faith and believe the worst. Tragedy's blinders affected Christ's followers, and they forgot Jesus's words that death wouldn't be the end of heaven's story.

> Jesus began to show his disciples that he must go to Jerusalem and undergo great suffering at the hands of the elders and chief priests and scribes, and be killed, and on the third day be raised.
> —MATTHEW 16:21

What everyone, including Satan, somehow overlooked is that Jesus came to beat the grave! Death had to happen so that a glorious resurrection could follow. And it did! We know that three days after His burial Christ did what no other king or political leader could do: He burst open that tomb and forever conquered the consequences of sin!

You see, the cross is the greatest "gotcha" in history. In his nearsightedness Satan thought he had led the Lamb to His slaughter, but he actually led himself into a divine trap devised even before the world was founded. What was once the highest tool of Roman execution and the surest means of silencing became the symbol of life and victory! At Christ's cross Satan was instantly stripped of all the power he once used to enslave humanity, incite fear, and rule creation. The effects of sin—the guilt, shame, and that record of wrongs—were all rendered powerless by the selfless sacrifice of the Son of God.

> He stripped all the spiritual tyrants in the universe of
> their sham authority at the Cross and marched them
> naked through the streets.
> —COLOSSIANS 2:15, THE MESSAGE

We've all had that dream of going about our normal routine, maybe in class or at the office, when we realize we're stark naked and are suddenly mortified at the realization that everyone can see *everything*. It's the ultimate feeling of embarrassment, shame, and disgrace. And that's the image Scripture depicts of Satan's defeat. Christ's cross exposed him to the world for the fraud he is. It disrobed him of his knockoff uniform and placed him under heaven's authority. With this, Jesus said, "Gotcha, devil!" What Satan thought had defeated Jesus actually defeated him instead.

You Are Not Finished!

A few months prior to writing this I was called into an emergency Friday night prayer meeting regarding some significant spiritual warfare taking place with a friend's son. The devil had really taken hold of this boy, and his parents were crying out for help. Hearing of the seriousness, we immediately gathered at least fifteen people for prayer and to form a strong bond to stand against these attacks.

I encouraged the group that what the devil was using to try and defeat this boy would actually defeat the devil... *if we would take it to the cross*. And that's what we did. We declared the cross as our source of victory and reminded Satan of his defeat. Shortly thereafter the Spirit of the Lord flooded the room in a very tangible way. People began to sob, prophetic words were spoken, and hands were laid upon others who suddenly wanted more of God. It was an incredible sight to see, especially amongst such an eclectic group of people from various churches, many of whom had never encountered God to the depths that we went that evening.

Toward the end of the night I asked them to consider what had just happened. In one evening more than fifteen people encountered greater depths of God and were impassioned to take this back to their churches, which they did! Some later experienced the baptism of the Holy Spirit. Others began Sunday school classes on the subject of spiritual warfare, which in turn freed more people. One thing is for certain: no one in that original group is the same. This all happened because Satan began to attack one person, and we took it to the cross. I bet the devil wishes he'd never messed with that boy!

Satan sets up his attacks intending to take us down his road to our defeat. This was the goal of the accusations launched at me, and this is his goal for all of the junk that you've been through too. He wants to use your tragedy to blind you to hope, to make you think it's the end, and prepare you for your burial.

But this isn't God's final answer. God's plan since the foundation of the world is the cross. It was for Jesus, and it is for you and me too. He wants you to go to the place of victory where He declares, "It is finished!" Here the habits that you couldn't break are finished, those seemingly unforgivable regrets are finished, and the accusations of the enemy are finished. At the cross sin's consequences are finished, *but you are not finished!* All the things Satan has used to try and defeat you will actually defeat him. Those things that were once the marks of shame and sorrow will become signs of new life. The cross still says, "Gotcha, devil!"

The reason you're reading this book isn't coincidence. It's because God's plan is pursuing you! He's committed to your resurrection—to a life that's healed, above the influence of Satan, and with a story that frees many others. He wants your testimony to be, "What Satan meant for harm, God has turned in to good!" (See Romans 8:28.)

But resurrection only happens on the other side of the cross. Up until now we've beheld it, marveled at it, and stood beside it, but we haven't gotten up on it. You can't experience a truly victorious life until you've followed Christ in your own crucifixion. You've chosen the way of the cross, so to the nails you must go...

Chapter 8

NO LOITERING!

I N MY HOMETOWN THERE'S A CITY PARKING LOT
that was famous for attracting riffraff. In the evenings you'd
drive by and see numerous people standing around, mostly
up to no good. It was a real nuisance for the city until they
posted a sign that warned, "No Loitering!"

> **loiter**—stand or wait around idly or without apparent
> purpose[1]

"No Loitering" signs are often used in public places to keep
people from persistently "hanging out" with no purpose. I
really believe that the sign should also be read at our altars
today. In other words, many of us come to Christ and just
gawk at, wait around, or stand idly by the cross. "Oh! What a
wonderful cross. What a sacrifice!" we marvel. But that's not
enough to silence Satan and live victoriously. We can't loiter at
the cross; we must get on it ourselves! This is what Jesus meant
when He instructed that we take up our own crosses.

> If any want to become my followers, let them deny
> themselves and take up their cross and follow me. For

those who want to save their life will lose it, and those who lose their life for my sake will find it.

—MATTHEW 16:24–25

Getting up on the cross—this is the place where Satan's accusations finally forced me. When he confronted me, I'd been in some form of ministry for more than five years, held a couple of leadership roles, and was attending seminary. I was immersed with Christianity, to say the least, but at some point in all the hubbub of "professional ministry" I'd grown familiar with, maybe even numb to, the things that mattered most.

While I believed passionately in the power of God for victorious living, I wasn't completely living it myself. Beyond the lip service, my thought life was just as impure; I struggled with the same habits and maintained the same fears and insecurities as those without a Christian label. Satan's accusations were especially poignant because he reminded me of the things that I knew existed in me, which provided a great case for why I should "shut it all down."

In that moment I remember feeling hopeless. Over the years I tried nearly every method of spiritual warfare. I fasted, prayed in the Spirit, attended church events as often as the doors were open, went through deliverance curriculum, and even cleansed my apartment of things that might be "cursed." Even after every demon was rebuked, I still didn't have lasting victory! *"What more could I do?"* I thought.

Indeed, there was nothing more for me to do, which was what I had to come to realize. My efforts couldn't hold me in holiness, but Jesus would! Those methods that I'd previously attempted are great and have their place, but they're no substitute for the cross. I needed to die, and the cross was the key to finally dethroning Satan in my life.

Life After Death

As we know, Christ's crucifixion paved the way for His glorious resurrection. And that's God's design for our lives too. Jesus's call for us to join Him in crucifixion is so that a resurrected life can follow. He likens this to the experience of a seed, which must first undergo death in order to produce a harvest.

> I tell you the truth, unless a kernel of wheat is planted in the soil and dies, it remains alone. But its death will produce many new kernels—a plentiful harvest of new lives. Those who love their life in this world will lose it. Those who care nothing for their life in this world will keep it for eternity.
> —JOHN 12:24–25, NLT

Within a single seed is the potential for so much new life. Given the proper circumstances, it will sprout into a plant, which can then produce more seeds that sprout into more plants. That's a wonderful plan, but it's contingent upon a very uncomfortable process.

When a seed is dropped onto the ground, with the right amount of water, oxygen, and temperature, new life is birthed inside. As water is absorbed into the seed, its outer shell is softened so that when the seed is buried into the proper soil, the shell cracks open and the new life inside can emerge.[2]

Notice that the life held inside of the seed doesn't burst the shell open itself. Rather, the shell is first crushed so that the life may arise. Imagine if the seed never died. The potential inside of it would never be seen, and it would never have the ability to reproduce.

Do you see the tremendous parallels for your life? At salvation God plants His seed in you, and new life is birthed (See 1 John 3:9.). What's holding back your new life? Is it slavery to sin, guilt, shame, doubts, or feelings of worthlessness? These are the things that the outer shell of the seed represents, which must be cracked, crushed, and killed so that all of the potential in you can burst forth. When you follow Christ in crucifixion, you're finally set free from what's in the way of victorious living so that your life can help many others experience the same.

Consider Yourself Dead

There's no getting around that the way to life is the way of the cross. But it often gets a little vague from there. How and to what must we die? Certainly we can't follow Christ to a literal death, nor should we. Notice that Jesus didn't call us to take up His cross, but to take up our own. Our crucifixion is not physical, but rather it's death to the things that uniquely hold us back to fully live for God.

Before you get into the trap of thinking about what you must *do* to die to these things, remember that victory is not a result of your own efforts and striving. You can't crucify yourself with a bunch of rules and legalism. It's not about living a life of lack or adhering to a list of "can't haves." Don't live in fear of wearing nice clothes, having a good car, or enjoying some entertainment. "Taking up your cross" doesn't mean inflicting yourself with burdens. God's people lived under law for thousands of years, and Jesus came to set us free from this!

Here's the key point that you can't miss: Paul remarked that crucifixion happens *with* Christ (Gal. 2:19–20). That is, your crucifixion happened with Jesus's. Still, it's made effective in your life when you *consider* it.

> *Consider* yourselves dead to sin and alive to God in Christ Jesus.
>
> —ROMANS 6:11,
> emphasis added

Consider is crucial because it's an active word that means to "think carefully about." Remember, we said that Satan's playground is in the mind, so we must defeat him in the place he attacks. To consider yourself dead to sin is really a constant renewal of your mind according to what Jesus exclaimed is finished on the cross.

Notice also that Paul never taught that sin is dead, but that you're dead to sin. Sin will always have its lure, and just as soon as you lose sight of the cross, it will regain its appeal to you. I honestly believe this is what happens with most fallen ministers. At some point in ministry they lost sight of the cross, and their sin nature regained its power. Once that happens, it's game on for sin's crazy cycle and Satan's accusations.

The cross is an anchor for holiness, and when your mind remains fixed upon it, the things that once enslaved you or held you back aren't so influential. This is what being crucified is all about: you're dead to every power except Christ, who's alive in you! Isn't it freeing to know that your victory lies not in what you do but in what He's done? So, when sin or shame presents itself, cast it off by saying, "I'm dead to that," and give it no second thought.

Our Three Deaths

Throughout the Book of Galatians Paul reveals the three things that hold us back—the three things to which we must consistently consider ourselves dead: our self, our flesh, and the world.

Crucifixion of self

Our *self* is our person. It's who we are. And who we are is a product of various situations and circumstances, including family history, life experiences, successes and failures, and hopes and disappointments. These things become the filters by which we live our present lives and see the future. Much of the issues we face are related to *self*, which is why it's often said that we're our own worst enemy.

If there was anyone who understood everything involved in giving up his old self, it was Paul. He was the son of parents respected amongst the establishment. His education was top notch. He was a Pharisee of Pharisees (Acts 23:6)! Certainly he enjoyed a rather stellar reputation. But when confronted by Christ, he had to give it all up. Paul understood that in order to attain the life and fulfill the call that Jesus promised, he had to get his *self* out of the way.

> I have been crucified with Christ; and it is no longer I who live, but it is Christ who lives in me.
> —GALATIANS 2:19–20

Crucifixion of self can be a slow and difficult death because it involves exalting Christ's finished work above *all* the various aspects of your life. *Who you were, who you are,* and *who you plan to be* must all be transformed into what God says about your past, present, and future. Let's *consider* some of these from the vantage point of the cross.

Consider yourself dead to your **past**.

Paul wrote that he wanted to know Christ and the power of His resurrection, so that he too might experience this resurrected life (Phil. 3:9). The key to this, he challenged, is to forget the past.

> But this one thing I do: forgetting what lies behind and straining forward to what lies ahead, I press on toward the goal for the prize of the heavenly call of God in Christ Jesus.
> —PHILIPPIANS 3:13–14

This prize that Paul spoke of was the call of God and the incredible future that God had planned. In order to have this, however, he had to train his mind to disregard the past and consider himself dead to it. He did so by holding fast to everything he attained because of the finished work at Christ's cross (v. 16).

Remember that Jesus was wounded for our transgressions, crushed for our iniquities, and by His bruises we are healed (Isa. 53:5). The cross paid for all the regrets and pain of the past, whether a result of your own sin or someone else's. Part of the resurrected life is that the Lord transforms the dirty things that once haunted you with shame and regret into something beautiful (Isa. 61:1–3).

Your former life is nailed to the cross and you're declared an "oak of righteousness," which displays God's grandiosity (v. 3). When Satan whispers to remind you of these things in an attempt to make you feel worthless or guilty, consider that you're healed, made beautiful, and adorned with the glory of God. Cast down those nagging thoughts and say, "I'm dead to you."

Consider yourself to dead to your **present**.

As I've said, who you are today is often a product of former circumstances and situations. The trap of Satan is that he wants you to identify with those things and believe that who you were is who you'll always be. He'll give flashbacks of the past that cause your emotions to react with feelings of insecurity, depression, anger, and so on.

With a past of rejection, I was so used to people laughing at me. So into my early adulthood, if I walked into a room and saw people laughing in the corner, I'd flash back to childhood and assume they must be laughing at me. "This is what's always happened; this is what's still happening," I thought. With this, I'd get insecure and very quiet. For too many years

I allowed my past to dictate my present and play puppeteer to my emotions.

Be careful not to filter your present circumstance through experiences you've been through. It only contaminates your life and makes you even more vulnerable to the devil. Are you gripped by any of the following feelings or emotions?

◊ Anger

◊ Confusion

◊ Depression

◊ Fear

◊ Guilt

◊ Jealousy

◊ Pride

◊ Sadness

◊ Rejection

Your struggle with any of these (or others) is likely related to things you've gone through or what someone else has said. From personal experience I know that victory in this area only happens with the renewal of the mind according to Christ's victory. Consider today from the vantage point of the cross: You're accepted, righteous, and made worthy because of the blood of Jesus. It's a new day, and you have a brand-new start!

Consider yourself to dead to your **future**.

The first disciples of Jesus—Peter, James, and John—made their livings as fishermen. In fact, they were about their business when Jesus first called to them. "Put out into the deep water and let down your nets for a catch," Jesus instructed

(Luke 5:4). Peter wasn't too excited to do this because he had just begun to clean up from an unsuccessful all-night fishing trip. Still, at Christ's command, he let down his net. Suddenly the net began to fill and fill with so many fish that it was about to break. Jesus said to the fishermen, "Do not be afraid; from now on you will be catching people" (v. 10). With this, Peter and his partners immediately left their fishing jobs to follow Jesus.

Notice what happened to these first disciples: Jesus didn't call them away from their passions, but He transformed their passions for His purposes. They were fishermen, but following Christ, they fished for men. God used the interests and talents with which He gifted them from birth for His glory. Furthermore, when they followed His command, the Lord turned an unsuccessful venture into a huge catch!

My story is similar to that of these first followers. From my youth I always loved things to do with technology. I have worked in the industry since a teenager and was often blessed with jobs that were the envy of my peers. Everyone expected me to be a successful programmer or designer. And those were my plans too. I looked forward to a life of accomplishment and wealth, laced with plenty of luxury.

But at my salvation God planted a new passion in me for His Word and His church. As time went on, these newfound desires didn't wane; they intensified. Eventually I had to make a decision: continue down the road of my own plans or accept the future the Lord had ordained. As I struggled with the options, I found the most satisfaction in ministry work. And so it was as if I followed Peter, James, and John into the deep water and dove in over my head to follow Jesus.

My acceptance of God's call didn't suddenly erase my talents and interests. I'm still a sucker for gadgets and anything digital. I can still spend hours in a tech store or surfing hobbyist blogs. But rather than use my talents for my own benefit,

I use them for God's. My ministry began largely through media, including television and Internet, and even mobile apps. Following Jesus didn't mean I was called away from my passions, but God made my passions more meaningful.

As He said to His first disciples, Jesus says the same to you: "Do not be afraid!" God won't take you away from something just to leave you miserable. His plan for you is highly satisfying.

> "For I know the plans I have for you," says the LORD.
> "They are plans for good and not for disaster, to give
> you a future and a hope."
> —JEREMIAH 29:11, NLT

God's road map for your life is so much better than anything you could devise—it's a future filled with hope and promise! Still, you must choose it on your own. Jesus said, "No one can serve two masters.... You cannot serve God and wealth" (Matt. 6:24). If you're straddling the line between your plans and God's, it's time to make a decision. I'm not suggesting that you leave your job. Certainly not everyone is meant for so-called platform ministry. But you are meant to be a *minister* in your everyday life.

In whatever employment or circumstances you find yourself, Jesus asks that you leave your ambitions and take on His. Will you embrace trust instead of trepidation? Giving rather than greed? Significance versus success? Fruit over finance? Mission above money? Die today to your future and receive Jesus's: an abundant, resurrected life that makes a difference in the lives of many others.

Crucifixion of flesh

The *flesh* is the influence in us that consistently seeks our own passions and desires instead of the things of God. You might think of it as the great manufacturer of sin. Its power is always at work in the parts of your body (Rom. 7:23), pumping out wrong thoughts and regretful actions.

> When you follow the desires of your sinful nature, the results are very clear: sexual immorality, impurity, lustful pleasures, idolatry, sorcery, hostility, quarreling, jealousy, outbursts of anger, selfish ambition, dissension, division, envy, drunkenness, wild parties, and other sins like these.
> —GALATIANS 5:19–21, NLT

The flesh is often attractive to your senses and may appear fun and liberating. This is what enticed Eve in the garden. When she looked to see that the fruit was pleasant to her eyes, she fell victim to the flesh. Its influence is great and is possibly Satan's deadliest trap against you. As we saw in chapter 1, after you yield to the passions and desires he presents to your body, he then swoops in with his usual accusations.

Many of us find ourselves in a daily wrestling match between the pleasures of the flesh and the fruits of God. The Bible reveals that when the flesh is alive and active, it'll always be at odds with the Spirit, keeping you from the resurrected life that Jesus died to give.

> The sinful nature wants to do evil, which is just the opposite of what the Spirit wants. And the Spirit gives us desires that are the opposite of what the sinful nature desires. These two forces are constantly fighting each other, so you are not free to carry out your good intentions.
> —GALATIANS 5:17, NLT

You must know that the flesh can never be transformed. It's corrupt at its core, and there's simply no way to redeem it. The only solution to overcome its power is to kill it with the nails of Christ's cross.

> Those who belong to Christ Jesus have nailed the passions and desires of their sinful nature to his cross and crucified them there.
> —GALATIANS 5:24, NLT

The power of the cross in your life is the key to silencing Satan and living victoriously! As Paul revealed, it's the authority with which we come against the flesh, and it's the means by which we weaken its influence.

> Put on the Lord Jesus Christ, and *make no provision for the flesh*, to gratify its desires.
> —ROMANS 13:14, emphasis added

To make a provision for something is to provide resources for its growth or activity. Fuel for your car is provision for it to operate; food is provision for your life. To win the war over your flesh, it's essential to suffocate and starve it.

Computer scientists know of the "garbage in, garbage out" principle. Basically, if you input junk data into a computer, the computer will spit out junk data. This principle is in affect for you and me too. What you entertain with your thoughts, eyes, and ears will eventually find its way out of you. If your life seems more like garbage out, it's probably because you're letting garbage in.

Satan studies the lures that cause you to stumble and counts upon these to keep you ensnared. To consider yourself dead to sin is an active process of looking away from these things. If surfing the Internet in the evening is an issue, then you must find a way to avoid this. If crude talk or jokes corrupt your thoughts, leave the conversation or make it clear that you won't tolerate it. If a magazine, billboard, Internet ad, or television commercial might put your mind in the wrong place, immediately look away, click away, or change the channel. Think, "I'm dead to that," and entertain it no longer.

To live victoriously, you must get radical about eliminating the garbage that enters your mind, eyes, and ears. And it's essential that you're proactive about it. If you wait until you're tempted, it's usually too late.

What you behold is what you desire. Whatever you gaze on is what you become. Don't commit your gaze to anything less than Jesus. Dethrone the power of the flesh by keeping your mind at Christ's cross, washed in His blood, and thus pierced by the nails of crucifixion.

Crucifixion to the world

The apostle John wrote that we shouldn't love the world's ways or the world's goods (1 John 2:15). *The world*, according to John, is one big system of greed—"wanting your own way, wanting everything for yourself, wanting to appear important" (v. 16, THE MESSAGE). This system is the last of what Paul instructed we must die to at the cross.

> May I never boast of anything except the cross of our Lord Jesus Christ, by which the world has been crucified to me, and I to the world.
> —GALATIANS 6:14

Dead to things

A young religious ruler once approached Jesus to know the secret to the resurrected life. "What must I do to inherit eternal life?" the man inquired (Luke 18:18). Though he was faithful to the law since his youth, Jesus revealed there was a greater test this ruler had yet to pass. It was the *things test*. "Sell all that you own and distribute the money to the poor," Jesus instructed, "...then come, follow me" (v. 22). Sadly, because the man couldn't give up his riches, he walked away from the resurrected life he sought.

What Jesus posed to the rich ruler wasn't to establish a new law that we should have nothing, but it was a motive checker to ensure nothing has us. Though many have made too much out of what Jesus meant, it's actually very simple: have what you can have and still keep Jesus first. Some people can handle great prosperity, and through it they are a blessing to many. Others can handle only a little. Where you fall in this spectrum is unique to you. The point Jesus made to the rich ruler wasn't a vow of poverty, but to give up anything that stands in the way of following Him.

Are you held captive to a love of things? If so, train your mind and actions through daily generosity. Tip your server more than is customary. Pay for someone's meal. Give an offering to your favorite church or ministry. Random acts of generosity will help to take your mind off yourself and keep you in control of your possessions, not your possessions in control of you.

Dead to people

One of the greatest loves that hold us back from victorious living is the unhealthy desire to please people. Most who love the world are actually enslaved to the protection of their reputation. Whether or not they follow Jesus is dependent upon the ever-changing opinions of those around them.

A rich tax collector named Zacchaeus wanted desperately to see Jesus, but two things stood in his way—himself and people. Zacchaeus was a short man, and his stature proved to be a significant hindrance in the swelling crowd. But those who are desperate for Jesus do desperate things. And Zacchaeus was determined that nothing would keep him from beholding the Lamb of God. So rather than concede to the crowds, he climbed a tree and got above the crowds. His tenacity caught the attention of Jesus and led to the opportunity to spend personal time in Christ's presence (Luke 19:1–6).

Perhaps it's the people in your life—friends, family, or coworkers—who hold you back in your relationship with God. Are you afraid that people will ridicule your passion or mock your faith? Do you fear their questions? You'll never dine at the table of Christ, or take daring steps of faith, if you let people stand in your way.

Determine to be like Zacchaeus, and do whatever it takes to get above the crowds and their opinions. Pray in public. Respond to that altar call. Attend that small group. Invite your neighbor, coworker, or classmate to church. Small steps of boldness each day will help to bust your care of reputation and crack open the door to the victorious life that Jesus has for you.

$$\sim$$

Physical crucifixion was never instantaneous, but a long, slow, and painful process. And your crucifixion is no different. You spend years thinking about yourself, catering to your flesh, and living in a corrupt world. Don't feel defeated if you don't overcome these things overnight. Jesus said it's a process that must happen daily (Luke 9:23). The next section of this book is devoted to help you through this journey, day by day.

When I stopped loitering at the cross and got up on it, I *began* the process of renewing my mind according to the finished work of Jesus. It certainly doesn't mean that I never fall to sin, but that I now hold to the authority of the cross with which I resist Satan. As we've seen, the historical cross of Jesus is the place where the devil and his minions were disarmed (Col. 2:15). In the same way, only the nails of crucifixion will hold you in holiness and above the voice and influences of Satan.

When you're dead to yourself, your flesh, and the world, there are no grounds for Satan to work in your life, and there's nothing to hold back that new life of greatness planted inside of you.

Section III

LIVING IN VICTORY

Chapter 9

THE PLACE OF GOD'S DELIGHT

A NEWBORN BABY BURSTS FORTH FROM ITS mother's womb and instantly experiences an array of sensations. The trauma of being sandwiched through the birth canal, the sudden inflation of its tiny lungs with foreign air, the never-before-seen lights glowing through its paper-thin eyelids, and the abrupt change in temperature from 98.6 degrees to the chilled hospital room—all bring the infant to a shriek. In a little while the baby will partake in many of the most basic human functions; he or she will eat, sleep, breathe...*and crave.*

Yes, *crave.* Scientists inform us that shortly after an infant is born, he or she feels a profound longing for the milk of the mother's breast and the presence of the mother herself. A newborn "[seems] to know, beyond any doubt, that he or she [needs] something outside the self, in order to be complete," they say.[1]

Throughout life the child will grow to crave many things, from acceptance, love, and intimacy, to warm, gooey, fudge-drizzled brownies or Coca-Cola. A sense of desire is a fundamental part of the human experience, which, according to the experts, is a deeply rooted *understanding* from birth that there's a hole that needs to be filled.[2]

Though I don't believe science will ever fully understand the intricacies of God's design, it is slowing realizing what God's Word has said all along. Sure, some foolishly minimize our need for fulfillment as merely evolutionary instinct. But the Bible reveals the real reason. We didn't learn to crave something more through millions of years of survival of the fittest. No, it was instilled into humankind from our conception—from the moment God breathed His breath in us.

> Then the LORD God formed man from the dust of the ground, and breathed into his nostrils the breath of life; and the man became a living being.
> —GENESIS 2:7

God's *breath of life* was the final and most essential element in bringing humankind into existence. It remains the same for each life conceived today. Only with God's breath do we become living beings; His breath gives us our souls (v. 7, KJV).

The Hebrew word used here for "living being" (or "soul") is *nephesh*. Throughout Scripture it represents the totality of a person: mind, will, and emotions. We're considered whole only after God breathes something of Himself into us.

God's breath, however, is more than divine CPR, which thrusts us into life. *It is the source of our craving.* The soul that God's breath implants into us is programmed to forever yearn for Him. This is why David cried, "My soul thirsts for God," and again a bit later, "My soul clings to you" (Ps. 42:2; 63:8). In other words, David exclaimed, "Everything within me desires to hold tightly to You, God!"

For the time up until the Fall, Adam and Eve enjoyed a close, deep, everyday relationship with God. The Bible teaches that the first couple actually walked and talked with the Creator (Gen. 3:8). How awesome!

As we know well by now, like a pair of scissors taken to a broadband cable, their sin severed the always-on connection between God and man. They were evicted from the garden and would no longer enjoy fellowship with the Father and the benefits of His presence. Though much was lost at the Fall, God's breath remained in them and their descendants, and with it a persistent desire for Him.

What scientists describe as the sense that we're incomplete isn't something psychological, but rather it's something deeply seated within us from conception. God breathed into us souls that long for Him. For many it's subconscious, but nonetheless, it's an undergirding draw that lures us on a search to regain friendship with God. Some stop temporarily or completely, thinking they've found wholeness and fulfillment in something else, but those things are eventually fleeting, and the search continues. We can't help it; there's a breath in us that's not satisfied unless we draw near to our Creator.

The Way Back to Eden

People agonize to find "God's will" for a certain situation; it can be the subject of tremendous debate. "Is it God's will to heal?" many wonder. "Does He always desire to bless?" others ask. I never want to make light of these weighty questions or glaze over them with a pat answer, *but God's perfect will for you and me is found in Scripture.* It's Eden.

Think about it. The place He made for humankind before it was wrecked with sin was Eden. When He finished the creation week, He looked down at everything and saw "it was very good" (Gen. 1:31). Without sin, we'd still dwell in Eden.

One of my favorite "gems" of Scripture that I love to sit and ponder is "Eden" itself. Many of us pass over Eden as simply another name for a place, like St. Louis or Miami. But to those in Old Testament times, Eden held rich meaning. They read it as the *description* of a place, which means, "delight." Literally, Eden is "God's delight," "God's pleasure," or even "God's glory." These are all descriptions that represent "God's presence." God created humankind to live in the dwelling of His delight and His glory—a place of perfect health, complete provision, and intimacy with Him. Consider nothing less than these things for God's ultimate will for you.

It's no wonder Satan felt so threatened. He'd been kicked out of God's presence, and in his envy he wanted to ensure no one else enjoyed it. So his temptation and accompanying guilt were aimed to remove Adam and Eve from this place too. As we know, it worked. When evicted from the Garden of Eden, they were actually removed from God's presence. After all these years Satan's focus hasn't changed. His tactics are still intended to remove people from this place.

After the Fall, the remainder of the Bible contains the accounts of God's pursuit to bring His creation back into relationship with Him. Ultimately this is what the blood of atonement that we explored in chapter 6 is about. Through His law and the sacrifice of animals God established a way to have oneness with Him, at least temporarily. But He wasn't satisfied. All of creation was restless and groaned for something permanent, which would once and for all restore what was lost at the Fall (Rom. 8:19–22). Isn't this the longing we feel and the fundamental source of our own restlessness and dissatisfaction? Isn't this why you're reading this book? We were designed to be in a good-standing relationship with our Creator, not temporarily, but forever.

See Jesus again upon that cross. With the bellow "It is finished!" He just announces that His mission is complete and He can return home. He lifts His heavy head to heaven to give

His Father one last glance from His bloodshot, human eyes. Just as quickly He closes those eyes, takes a final gasp, and His head falls to His shoulders as He expires at about three in the afternoon.

Suddenly there's an earthquake that splits rocks and rolls open tomb doors. To the onlookers the moment declares that He was, in fact, the Son of God. But there's something so much grander. The temple curtain is torn in two, completely split from top to bottom (Matt. 27:51)!

The significance of this moment can't be missed. Perhaps beyond everything else, this is the moment that changes *every-thing*. The temple was the place long established to carry out the sacrifices for the yearly atonement. The Book of Hebrews describes its layout.

> For a tent was constructed, the first one, in which were the lampstand, the table, and the bread of the Presence; this is called the Holy Place. *Behind the second curtain was a tent called the Holy of Holies.* In it stood the golden altar of incense and the ark of the covenant overlaid on all sides with gold, in which there were a golden urn holding the manna, and Aaron's rod that budded, and the tablets of the covenant; above it were the cherubim of glory overshadowing the mercy seat.
> —HEBREWS 9:2–5,
> emphasis added

Behind the curtain inside the temple was the Holy of Holies—the place where the presence of God was said to reside. Once a year only the high priest could enter, and only with the perfect blood of a lamb by which his and the people's sins may be covered. The temple curtain was the quintessential symbol of sin's effects; it kept the people separated from their God, and God from His people.

Jesus, our High Priest, entered the Holy of Holies and shed His perfect blood for the covering of the world's guilt and shame once and for all! With this His mission was complete, and the Father's mighty hands grabbed that loathed curtain and sent it flying into two pieces.

The works of the devil were finally destroyed! God would no longer be contained behind the curtain inside a temple made by hands, but rather He moved into His new sanctuary—His people—where access to His presence may be enjoyed at any moment.

> We have confidence to enter the sanctuary by the blood of Jesus, by the new and living way that he opened for us through the curtain.
> —HEBREWS 10:19–20

The cross brought forgiveness of sin and the end of guilt and shame, which is huge enough. But it did even more. The cross restored the way back to Eden. Now, Christ is in you (Col. 1:27), and you have anytime access to the delight and glory of God's presence.

Life in God's Delight

One of the great (or not!) experiences about spending time with a friend is that you also spend time with his or her personality. If your friend is happy, you'll likely enjoy the sentiment. If he or she is agitated, on the other hand, you'll feel this too. This is why it's said that you are who your friends are. In other words, you take on the qualities and characteristics of those friends with whom you choose to spend your time.

In the same way, when we spend time with God, His personality begins to rub off on us. Those who make it a practice to commune with Him daily should begin to possess the evidence of His friendship, which are His fruit: love, joy, peace, patience, kindness, generosity, faithfulness, gentleness, and self-control (Gal. 5:22–23).

Rereading the Creation account according to what we now know about Eden brings out fascinating insight into all that God has for us through a resurrected life lived in His presence.

> And the LORD God planted a garden in [His delight], in the east; and there he put the man whom he had formed. Out of the ground [of His delight] the LORD God made to grow every tree that is pleasant to the sight and good for food, the tree of life also in the midst of the garden, and the tree of the knowledge of good and evil. A river flows out of [His delight] to water the garden, and from there it divides and becomes four branches.
>
> —GENESIS 2:8–10

Wow! Truly God formed us to dwell in His delight. Let's explore some of the benefits that we enjoy there.

All good things grow in God's presence.

When we think about things that are pleasant, we think of those things that bring happiness and satisfaction—probably things that make us feel complete and whole. When we think about things that support life, we consider the essentials such as food, water, and rest. The passage above reveals that out of the ground of God's presence all of these good things—pleasant and full of life—are grown. David experienced this. He said that in God's presence is "fullness of joy" and "pleasures forevermore" (Ps. 16:11). Anyone who has the habit of spending time in God's presence daily knows this to be true for his or her life too.

Any idea that I ever had that made an impact for the

kingdom of God was first conceived out of time with God. When I was just in high school, the Lord gave me a vision for a Christian conference to benefit the students of our school and the members of our community. I remember the first sleepless night when I talked and developed this idea with God for hours. It was invigorating and filled me with passion! A *good thing* was conceived that night in His presence, and when birthed, it impacted literally thousands in our community.

It doesn't always have to result in big vision or something to do, but rather time with God provides the proper attitude and the strength you need to take on the day. I've become fairly fanatical about waking up as early as 4:30 a.m. so that I can spend the best part of my day with the Lord. I learned that if I roll out of bed at 7:30 a.m., I have just enough time to scarf down breakfast and try to look good before I rush into the office. This only sets the wrong tone for the rest of the day.

When I awake early, however, I *enjoy* time to eat, exercise, and a relationship with God where I read, write, talk with, and simply listen to Him. This makes a tremendous difference in my day! I'm more peaceful, and I have greater confidence, a bigger smile, and even better ideas. Furthermore, it's as if I've feasted on something that gives me the strength and energy to face whatever comes my way. I certainly don't mean to imply that you must spend all night or awake early in order to be with God, but find *some* time every day to be with Him.

Far too many people feel incomplete, dissatisfied, restless, or suffer from a bad attitude. They try to ease these emotions in a variety of ways, yet nothing lasts for too long. In many cases perhaps these symptoms are the soul simply longing for the place it was designed to dwell. So rather than self-medicate, plant yourself in God's presence and experience the growth of good things in your life.

Refreshment flows from God's presence.

One morning at five o'clock I found myself particularly weary from so many deadlines that I needed to meet and so many projects that appeared to have little progress. I've learned that I don't do so well with mounting to-dos because my mind tends to constantly try and resolve those things that have no closure. Needless to say, the early part of my prayer time that morning seemed nearly useless. I simply couldn't focus on getting still before the Lord, and my thoughts drifted from worry to worry.

But time in the presence of the Lord is never wasted. God understands our weaknesses; He experienced many of the same trials and temptations that we do (Heb. 4:15). So He offers us to come to Him for comfort. In this moment I heard Jesus speak to me through Scripture: "Come to me, all you that are weary and are carrying heavy burdens, and I will give you rest. Take my yoke upon you, and learn from me; for I am gentle and humble in heart, and you will find rest for your souls. For my yoke is easy, and my burden is light" (Matt. 11:28–30).

At some point in my busy schedule I had forgotten that the Spirit of God inside of me is the helper and the comforter. He is the advocate, which supports me. I had taken the tasks of ministry upon myself and made them difficult and burdensome. Jesus had to remind me to give it to Him. "Come to me, Kyle," He said. "I will give you rest and refreshment to your soul."

Refreshment. That's what I found that morning in His presence. It was like I simply laid my head on the chest of Jesus and was finally still. "It's going to be OK," He encouraged. "Let's do this *together.*" This single moment with Him changed the day. What began with weariness ended with rejuvenation. In His presence He poured the living water of His Spirit upon me, which moistened my dryness and resurrected my passion.

In the refreshment of God's presence is where we were always meant to live. According to the Creation story, a river flowed out of His delight in order to refresh the garden (Gen. 2:10). Even more, the river divided into more rivers that refreshed the lands around it. Will you come to Jesus today and experience the rivers of living water that flow from His presence? You'll be so filled and satisfied that not only will you be refreshed, but also you'll be refreshment to those around you!

Purpose is found in God's presence.

"Why am I here? What's my purpose?" These two "great philosophical worldview questions" are ones that we all ask from time to time. On more than one occasion I've found myself on my knees begging God for the answers. So have you, I'm sure.

We all want to feel like we're consuming earth's resources for a purpose. We all want to feel needed and important. So we look to *things* to define our identities and purposes. We find them in accomplishments and successes. We place them in other people.

In my early adulthood I had tremendous opportunities in the political world, and I began to place much of my value in all of this. I had led a large political group at my university and later worked on some esteemed campaigns where I hobnobbed with some of the world's greatest political figures and business leaders. Remember, much of my childhood was filled with rejection, so it felt great to finally be considered "important."

As seasons in life do, this one too passed. I began to notice that the photos that adorned my wall from those "glory days" were looking older and older and the memories more distant. It was a hard transition to the next season in life, and I often wondered if God had just set me on a shelf. No longer shaking hands with presidents, I questioned if my best days were behind me.

But purpose, worth, and identity aren't found in the things

of this world; they're found in Jesus. Time in His presence not only reveals to you purpose, but it also rises up passion. The ministry I lead today was conceived in no other way than day after day listening and talking to the still, small voice of God. And I promise you, God doesn't shout; He whispers. So you must get in close!

But even in "ministry" we must be careful that its tasks don't define us. Jesus didn't die to set us on a treadmill of things to do, as world changing as they may be. He came to restore the relationship with God for which we were primarily created. Notice the charge God gave to Adam:

> The LORD God took the man and put him in the garden of [His delight] to till it and keep it.
> —GENESIS 2:15

God's task to Adam was to purely "keep" His presence. Humankind was created for the simple purpose to be friends with God! Jesus endured the agony of the cross to bring us back to this place.

Check marks on your to-do list don't determine your value. The number of heads bowed at the altar call doesn't either. To be God's friend is His greatest purpose for you! And if you do nothing else in life, that's enough.

Healing happens in God's presence.

David's psalm about the divine Shepherd is a favorite among many Christians.

> The LORD is my shepherd, I shall not want. He makes me lie down in green pastures; he leads me beside still waters; he restores my soul.
> —PSALM 23:1–3

The first of David's words reveal refreshment in God's presence. In essence, he says, "Because God is near, I have everything that I need—plenty of food, ample water, and rest." The next line is especially poignant: "He restores my soul." Remember, Scripture often uses the word *soul* to represent the totality of a person: mind, will, and emotions. In other words, "He restores everything about me," David says.

I frequently refer to God's presence as an "incubator for the soul." An incubator is a machine that provides a warm, controlled environment for eggs to hatch or premature babies to develop. It serves as a great image of God's presence. When you spend time with Him, you enter an environment suitable for healing and growth. As we've already said, passion bubbles up in you, peace envelops your worried mind, gifts develop, and you begin to hear the truths that He says about you: "Worthy! Accepted! Righteous!"

If your mind needs healing from regrets and reminders of the past, fears of the future, or present negativity, the presence of God will restore peace. If your will needs to be conformed to His, allow God's hands to do the molding. Those in an emotional frenzy come to Jesus, drink in His living water, and find refreshment and calm. God desires to restore everything about you; this is the resurrected life!

Satan stays silenced in God's presence.

David continues his psalm with words of faith regarding the protection that He finds in the Lord.

> Even though I walk through the darkest valley, I fear no evil; for you are with me; your rod and your staff— they comfort me. You prepare a table before me in the presence of my enemies.
> —PSALM 23:4–5

Likely writing this in the midst of battle, David claims he has nothing to fear because God is with him. How I wish I could have such faith at times!

David didn't lament that he would be stuck in a dark valley; instead, he had the confidence that he would come out the other side on God's side! These words should comfort us to know that, *with God*, we can go *through* whatever we have to and come out victorious, without falling to the fiery darts of the evil one.

I especially love the imagery David portrays in the final line: a table prepared in the presence of his enemies. Imagine this: In God's presence is a long banquet table with the greatest feast you've ever seen. It's adorned with the freshest salads, finest meats, and most delectable desserts. This alone is heaven! You look outside to see the enemy salivating, mouthing things, and licking his lips. He'd love nothing more than to ravage the feast, but he can't get in and his taunting can't be heard.

The apostle James understood the presence of God as a place of spiritual warfare as well.

> Submit yourselves therefore to God. Resist the devil, and he will flee from you. Draw near to God, and he will draw near to you.
> —JAMES 4:7–8

The key to resisting the devil, James wrote, is to first submit to God. Come close to Him, and then He and the benefits of His presence will come close to you. The only way you enter God's presence is through Christ's sacrifice, and so when you're in it, you're actually covered in His blood. This paralyzes Satan and keeps him silenced in your life.

It's in You!

The benefits of God's presence are fathomless, and it's a particular passion of mine to write about them. David was so convinced of these things that he ends the psalm committed to living in God's presence for the rest of his life (Ps. 23:6). *Living in God's presence* is my goal, and it should be yours too. It's the only place where your soul will finally find the completeness it longs for. It's the place of resurrection that Jesus died to give you.

"But it's not realistic," some argue, "to be cooped up in prayer all day. We have to step out and face the world from time to time." This is Old Testament thinking! Yes, we can have profound encounters with God in our prayer closets or church sanctuaries, but it's not because these places are the source of God's presence themselves. But rather it's because we—the houses of God's Spirit—are in those places! The curtain was ripped to move God's presence out of a single place and into you, me, and all of those who accept Jesus as Lord.

I've seen tremendous healings and deliverances with my own eyes, but I still consider the greatest miracle is that the Creator of the universe lives in us. "Christ in you [is] the hope of glory," Paul exclaimed (Col. 1:27). Yes! There's no greater hope. Because of this we may enter God's presence boldly and at any time and in any place.

Time with God really doesn't have to be complicated or ritualized. Undoubtedly it's great to have a particular time and place to meet with the Lord, just as a favorite date location with your spouse. But relationship with God is meant for everyday life. Begin wherever you are with a simple prayer: "God, I want to meet with You." Then simply talk with Him while driving to work or school, brushing your teeth, with your head on the pillow, folding laundry, or as you enter a difficult situation.

You were designed for friendship with God; this is what your soul craves. Daily time with Him is paramount to living an overcomer's life; it will restore everything about you.

Chapter 10

THE UNIFORM
OF THE RIGHTEOUS

IR, SIR, COULD I JUST ASK YOU TO SWITCH BAGS
with your hands?" a man curiously pleads with a shopper
whose both hands are full of groceries. The shopper,
befuddled by the request, continues to his car and pays no
more attention to this apparent trickster. As every attempt is
captured on hidden camera, one by one the man tries to coerce
passersby in a shopping center parking lot to do incredibly
bizarre things. "Could you just go over and touch that brick?"
he implores another shopper casually strolling by. "No, no, no,"
the shopper, obviously annoyed, retorts as he scurries off.

The man is an actor conducting an experiment to test the
obedience of common folks on the street. His first test results
in what's expected. He is dressed as an average Joe, with no
signs of authority, and people treat him as just another crazy
and give his requests no second thought.

This all changes, however, as soon as he slips on a uniform.
It's rather humorous, actually. At the same shopping center,
this time outfitted in a security guard's uniform, the man
successfully convinces a woman with hands full of groceries

to walk squarely in a path around him and a random apple lying about twelve feet away. He convinces another shopper to throw a candy wrapper on the ground. Others give in to completely change the way they walk—to start out on the left foot instead of the right—and march slowly to their cars.

The experiment, as wacky as it sounds, reveals that authority isn't necessarily exuded from an individual himself or herself. It's often conveyed, rather, through numerous things, especially the outfit of the individual. In each test the same man made the same zany requests but, depending on his appearance, with dramatically different results. Dressed as a common man on the street, he was unsuccessful. When he was in a uniform particularly noted for its authority, however, people followed his directions nearly without question.

Other more scientific studies validate what this actor found to be true: there's power in a uniform. From a very young age we learn that certain uniforms convey authority, and throughout life we almost instinctively obey whoever wears them.[1]

The Chain of Command

All of creation exists within God's established hierarchy. He sits alone at the top of His organization chart, followed by the angels, and finally, a little lower yet, are you and me (Ps. 8:5; Heb. 2:7). God is the Most High, the beginning and the end; there's no higher power than His majesty. An understanding and respect of His authority are woven into creation, so that it's instinctive. When He speaks, mountains quake and hills lie down; knees bow in His presence, whether they want to or not.

As God in the flesh, the presence of Jesus radiates His authority too. In one story two demons immediately recognized Him and asked, "What have you to do with us, Son of God? Have you come here to torment us before the time?" (Matt. 8:29). Jesus didn't have to tell them who He was or even persuade them to leave. The demons instinctively knew that His presence carries the weight of God's authority so that when He said, "Go!", they instantly obeyed.

In the lowliness of Jesus's death on the cross, His name was raised to carry the authority of who He is and what He did.

> And being found in human form, he humbled himself and became obedient to the point of death—even death on a cross. Therefore God also highly exalted him and gave him the name that is above every name, so that at the name of Jesus every knee should bend, in heaven and on earth and under the earth, and every tongue should confess that Jesus Christ is Lord, to the glory of God the Father.
> —PHILIPPIANS 2:7–11

The work completed on the cross is all given an identity in the name of Jesus. Forgiveness *is* Jesus. Deliverance *is* Jesus. Salvation *is* Jesus. Healing *is* Jesus. And so on. This is why it's often so powerful to simply pray, "Jesus." Just a whisper of His name has more power than any amount of words we can string together. His name represents ultimate victory! Devils, circumstances, and symptoms—any named thing—must bow at the mention of the name of Jesus.

I hope this isn't a major revelation to you, but *you are not God.* You and I must understand our place in the chain of command. Our presence alone doesn't move anything. Naturally, we're like the actor in the story above, rather weak, with nothing that intimidates Satan into doing anything we say.

Still, God has not left us in a state to be the devil's doormat. He's chosen to give us access to His power and authority, and He did it through Jesus's death. We know that when an individual dies, inheritance is left to beneficiaries, which are often his or her children. As believers, you and I are considered children of God.

> But to all who received him, who believed in his name,
> he gave power to become children of God.
>
> —JOHN 1:12

God's children are the legal beneficiaries of everything that He gave to Jesus (Eph. 1:11). At Calvary this inheritance was deposited into the accounts of all those who would later go there to receive it. So while we possess little in and of ourselves, those of us in Christ have access to so much more. This includes ownership in Jesus's name and the right to invoke its authority "over all the power of the enemy" (Luke 10:19).

As if staking a claim on a piece of land, put your foot down to the devil today and identity yourself: "I am a child of God!" Watch Satan flee, as he must obey the authority given to you through the name and presence of Jesus.

The Clothing of Christ

At the cross Jesus gave up His clothing and hanged naked before the world. The soldiers on the ground grabbled for a piece of His garment and eventually divided its articles amongst themselves (John 19:23). They wanted a little piece of this scorned man as a trophy to what they did that day.

But the clothing of Christ was worth so much more than the soldiers could have ever imagined. His clothing is His identity and represents everything that He is. Though the soldiers each grabbed a piece of His earthly attire, Jesus left the garment of who He is at the cross so that you and I would go there and put on the entirety of His identity.

> For you are all children of God through faith in Christ
> Jesus. And all who have been united with Christ in
> baptism have put on Christ, like putting on new
> clothes.
> —GALATIANS 3:26–27, NLT

I like to think of putting on Christ in the same way as putting on a uniform. Like those of police officers or servicemen and women, a uniform identifies the places they've been and the efforts they've made there. When in uniform these individuals possess the authority of the law to do things such as stop traffic or make an arrest. Without the uniform, however, they're left to rely on their own strength, which is considerably less powerful. Similarly those of us who have Christ as our uniform exude the power and authority from the victory He won at the place He went. Without this uniform we're powerless, but in it we can get the devil to do backflips!

Writing from a Roman prison, Paul observed Roman soldiers moving about in their armored uniforms. The soldier's uniform would have been very familiar to the first-century readers, so Paul used it as a way to relate what Christians possess in the Lord.

> Finally, be strong in the Lord and in the strength of
> his power. Put on the whole armor of God, so that you
> may be able to stand against the wiles of the devil. For
> our struggle is not against enemies of blood and flesh,
> but against the rulers, against the authorities, against
> the cosmic powers of this present darkness, against
> the spiritual forces of evil in the heavenly places.
> —EPHESIANS 6:10–12

An atheist once commented to a Facebook post I made about God's armor. "If God is *so* loving, why does He use language of weapons and warfare?" he asked with a bit of mockery. His question represents the wrong image many of us have of the whole armor of God. We've equated it with the armor of the world, made to engage in hand-to-hand combat. But God's armor isn't the armor of humans (2 Cor. 10:4). His armor is counter to anything of this world; it's armor of light with weapons of righteousness (Rom. 13:12; 2 Cor. 6:7).

Notice that Paul instructs to *be* strong and to find strength *in* the Lord's power so that you may *stand*. He doesn't say to put on the armor in order to fight, but that *in the Lord* you may maintain the standing of your identity in Christ against evil forces that seek destroy it. We don't possess the armor of God to engage in a bloodbath against Satan, as if we have to defeat him ourselves. No, the full armor of God is the uniform of Christ, which helps us *stand* in the victory that He's already won.

With the imagery of a Roman soldier's armor Paul used its six pieces to relate incredible insight about what we possess in Christ: belt, breastplate, shoes, shield, helmet, and sword. Let's explore how each of these things uniquely holds us in everything obtained at the cross.

The belt of truth

See the soldier's belt. It's a thick leather strap tied around his wool tunic. It's also referred to as a girdle because it's wide enough to cover the stomach and kidneys. Connected to it are bronze plates that hang down in order to protect the soldier's reproductive area. Of all the armor, the belt is the most foundational; it supports much of the other weaponry and is the only piece of the uniform worn at all times.

Paul likened this belt to the truth we have in Christ. "Stand therefore and fasten the belt of truth around your waist," he instructed (Eph. 6:14). Truth is what upholds everything about us. It's what grounds us so that we're able to stand strong in victory against the things that come against us. It's what keeps us forging onward, confident and secure in Christ.

The first area the belt protects is the stomach. The stomach, as we know, is the place that holds what we consume. As the body's great food processor, it mashes the food into digestible pieces, and its juices function to help kill bacteria in what was eaten.[2] We all know the feeling of an upset stomach. When we eat something that's really not good for us, a healthy stomach rejects it and gets it out of our bodies so that we aren't contaminated by it.

Satan, as the "father of lies," attempts to inject deceit in order to infect our lives. He wants you to take a bite of his fruit to send deception throughout your body so that your life becomes defeated. As they say, "You are what you eat." A constant diet of his lies will pervert your thinking until you identify yourself more with Satan's defeat than Christ's victory. If he can inject pity, you'll live pitifully. His fear planted within you is like a parasite that eats away at your confidence in God until you're paralyzed by doubts and what-ifs.

God wants you to get His truth within you because it's the only standard by which Satan's lies are rejected. If your life is girded by the truth of Christ, you know who you are in Him. You understand your worth made possible by His blood. When the devil slips his lies into your inward parts, they're immediately rejected and spewed out in the quickest ways possible.

God's truth also enables your life-giving organs to function. As we've already said, the greatest hindrance to being used by God is to believe that God can't use you. If Satan can convince you that you're too far gone or have messed up too many times to be used by God, then he has effectively sterilized your future from ever enjoying new life. "I can'ts," "I'm nots," and "I'll nevers" will immobilize you to stay within the box, never do anything daring, and never birth anything amazing. If your thinking and vocabulary are plagued by these excuses right now, get God's truth into you. Determine not to be satisfied with small things, but declare, "I can do all things through Christ who strengthens me" (Phil. 4:13, NKJV).

The devil would love to unfasten our belts, so that like Adam and Eve we stand naked and ashamed, hiding ourselves from God and cowering from the world. But the truth of Christ protects us from the tactics in Satan's playbook. It counters his lies and makes us certain of our identities in Christ. *Stand* in this truth today, digest it, and let it nourish your soul: "I'm accepted and made worthy by the blood of Jesus!"

The breastplate of righteousness

The soldier's breastplate provides a covering over each shoulder and the sides of the chest. It's possibly the most beautiful part of the armor. Scaled with many pieces of bronze or iron, it reflects the sun and glistens as the soldier moves about. The breastplate is so stunning, in fact, that it's hard to notice anything else in the uniform. It's heavy, though, possibly forty pounds or more. But the protection it provides over the heart and vital organs is worth its weight.

Paul revealed that the righteousness we have in Christ is like this soldier's breastplate (Eph. 6:14). It's a defensive piece of our uniform, for sure. It doesn't strike a blow to the enemy like a sword, but rather it simply covers and protects the most vital parts of who we are.

Throughout Scripture the word *heart* rarely refers to the blood-pumping organ that we know it as today. Instead it's most often used to describe the core being of a person. The biblical heart includes thoughts, emotions, spirituality, and any "inner" function of an individual. In other words, the heart is the essence of who we are. When David exclaimed, "I will give thanks to the LORD with my whole heart" (Ps. 9:1), he was saying, "I will give thanks to the Lord with everything in me."

Satan seeks to assault us at our core. Sure, he'll inflict physical pain at times, but he gets much more mileage attacking thoughts and influencing emotions. His whispers and accusations are aimed to corrupt the parts of your inner self in order to steal your identity and replace it with his defeated one. The moment you feel worthless or believe you're the worst Christian who's ever lived, he's successfully accomplished his mission.

Many Christians live defeated lives because they see themselves according to their old identities. They've forgotten, or possibly were never taught, that the cross provides an identity change. After the soldiers divided up Jesus's clothing, they then threw dice to see who would win His robe (John 19:23–24). Even in their mockery they understood its worth. Throughout Scripture the robe is identified as righteousness (Isa. 61:10). At the cross today we don't need to hope to obtain this robe through any effort or luck. No, God gives it to each of us freely.

Like the uniform that identifies the police officer, Christ's robe identifies you with everything that He is. Perhaps you've had problems seeing yourself in Christ. Allow me to hold up a mirror and describe how you appear to God: perfect, spotless, white, pure, holy, accepted, worthy, faultless, unblemished, among many other superlatives. Get this: you look like Jesus because you're covered in Him!

Satan can't do anything about this identity, because it's not about you but about Jesus, with whom he can find no fault. This is victorious living! See yourself adorned in the beauty and glamor of Christ's breastplate. Feel the weight of its protection and declare this now: "I am the righteousness of God in Christ Jesus" (2 Cor. 5:21).

The shoes of peace

The third piece of the armored uniform is the shoes. The soldier's shoes are actually a type of sandal, made of a thick leather sole embedded with bits of rock for better traction. The sandals are tied to the soldier's feet with numerous leather straps, and it's said that these shoes become more comfortable the more they are worn. Like every other piece of the armor, the shoes are designed for specific purpose: to keep the soldier planted while marching or standing in tumultuous soil.

Our feet are to be outfitted with the peace that comes from the gospel of Jesus Christ (Eph. 6:15). These "shoes of peace" provide us with the ability to go about our mission and into rough or unknown territories knowing that we won't slip. Like David, we can "walk *through* the darkest valley" and "fear no evil" (Ps. 23:4, emphasis added) because we have peace knowing that the victor will bring us out the other side, unharmed.

If you mistake peace as the absence of war, you'll be sorely disappointed. Jesus assured, "Here on earth you will have many trials and sorrows" (John 16:33, NLT). Tough times are part of the journey. We're not guaranteed well-traveled paths, that everyone will be nice to us, or that the devil won't try to mess with us. These are the facts of life.

Maybe you're a bit disappointed to hear this. "Trials and sorrows" don't seem like victorious living, do they? Yet Jesus said, "I have told you all this so that you may have peace in Me" (v. 33, NLT). "Peace in Me" is the most important part of what He said. In this world peace isn't found in our circumstances, but rather it's found *in* Christ. *In* Christ we have the refreshment and protection of His presence, which is peace. *In* Christ we also have peace with God, made possible by His righteousness.

We should find the ultimate comfort in Christ's final assurance. "But take heart," He said, "because I have overcome the world" (v. 33, NLT). Our greatest peace is founded upon the finished work of Jesus at the cross where He overcame sin's effects. Realize that this doesn't mean we won't live without sin's consequences. We're still in a fallen world where bad things happen. Sometimes we must deal with the unpleasant results of someone else's actions or our own. But Jesus rose above these things so that they couldn't hold Him back from resurrection.

In Christ you and I are made more than conquerors (Rom. 8:37), and with Him we're raised above the influences of the world. This is the resurrected life. You're raised above the effects of your past. Above all the junk that bombards your mind. Above the rejection or betrayal from friends and family. Above the disappointments of the things that didn't turn out as you hoped. Above the fear of how you'll meet the bills, whether or not you'll spend the rest of your life alone, or the chances of failure of your latest endeavor.

You must understand that peace doesn't simply happen; it's a decision you make. When you decide to rest in what Jesus accomplished on the cross, you'll enjoy an inner calm and tranquility in the midst of storms. Keep your mind focused on the victory of Christ, and you'll stand unmoved by whatever life brings. The more you do this, the more comfortable you'll be forging into unknown territory and rough situations.

The shield of faith

The soldier's shield can't be missed. It's a sizable article, about four feet tall by two and a half feet wide, put together by three pieces of curved laminate wood covered in leather. It's decorated with a large painted icon that represents the soldier's legion and a bronze rim around the edges. It's one of the more movable parts of the armor, designed to protect the soldier's entire body from arrows, swords, and javelins that might fly in from any direction.

In spiritual warfare the attacks of Satan come at us from all different directions. They're really unpredictable at times. The accusations he launched at me came without warning. One morning, going about my usual routine, I was broadsided with what Paul called Satan's "fiery arrows," which attempted to set fire to my identity in Christ.

The only thing that will block and extinguish these fiery arrows is a shield made of faith (Eph. 6:16). Scripture defines faith as "the confidence that what we hope for will actually happen...[the] assurance about things we cannot see" (Heb. 11:1, NLT).

Faith is the means by which we possess everything God has to offer. By faith we receive salvation and the assurance of it. By faith we believe God has forgiven us. By faith we receive the fullness of the Holy Spirit and His gifts. By faith we believe that God loves us and wants His best for us. When Satan calls your God-given dream, vision, prophetic word, or the written Word of God into question, the only recourse you have is to respond with confidence about what you can't or don't yet see.

While faith may be confidence in what you can't see, it isn't blind. If you look back into the pages of your life, I believe you'll see the evidence of God's faithfulness inked throughout. Hindsight picks up things in your life that often get overshadowed in the moment by your worried mind.

When I revisit the major events in my life, I clearly see a divine hand throughout, orchestrating my arrival and departure from place to place. With this in mind I gain renewed confidence that God will work out whatever situation I currently face. David's faith to defeat Goliath in battle came from remembering that God had previously helped him overtake a lion and a bear. You too will find that remembering God's goodness in the past is the key to confidence in the future.

The fact that you're here today reading this book means that the numerous things you once feared didn't destroy you. You have a Father who can be counted on to provide, protect, and finish what He started! Confidence in Him is your shield, and when you hold it high, your identity remains untouched from the darts of doubt, deception, or discouragement. "God's got this" will be your unwavering expectation.

The helmet of salvation

The soldier's crown is his helmet. It's a single piece of iron molded to fit upon his head, adorned with a peacock-like crest that makes it easy to identify his rank. Like today, head wounds in ancient times were the most common and fatal wounds of war. The plates that hang down along the sides and back protect his cheeks and the neck from the decapitating swing of the enemy's sword. The soldier wouldn't dare enter battle without his helmet.

Spiritually speaking, our heads represent what's in them—our minds. We have already established that the mind is Satan's playground. Our thoughts are the place we're the most vulnerable. With just a single notion dumped into our heads, Satan can effectively silence or shut us down. Paul understood just how much we're influenced by the mind, which is why he urged that we put on a helmet of salvation (Eph. 6:17).

Notice that Paul was writing this to the church at Ephesus. He wasn't speaking to unbelievers about making Jesus their Savior. Rather he was urging existing believers to deflect Satan's tactics by meditating on thoughts about the victory that saved them. He further expounds upon this to the Corinthians.

> For the weapons of our warfare are not merely human,
> but they have divine power to destroy strongholds.
> We destroy arguments and every proud obstacle

raised up against the knowledge of God, and we take
every thought captive to obey Christ.

—2 CORINTHIANS 10:4–5

The weapons we're given as a part of Christ's uniform help
us with our thinking. Satan barges into our lives with arguments as to why God can't use us, why we'll never be healed,
or why our particular sins are too big to be forgiven. These are
some of the doubts and discouragements he uses as obstacles
to keep us from a life of victory.

We may not be able to control what drops into our minds,
but we can take these thoughts captive by replacing them with
God's Word. Let's counter a few thoughts the devil may try
and inject with the knowledge about what we have in Christ.

Satan's Whisper	Knowledge of God
"God doesn't love you."	"For God so loved the world that he gave his only Son, so that everyone who believes in him may not perish but may have eternal life" (John 3:16).
"You've messed up too many times. You're too dirty to be used by God."	"So if anyone is in Christ, there is a new creation: everything old has passed away; see, everything has become new" (1 Cor. 5:17).
"The road ahead is too tough. You're never going to make it."	"For God has not given us a spirit of fear and timidity, but of power, love, and self-discipline" (2 Tim. 1:7, NLT).

It's so critical that we protect our minds with thoughts of
victory, because if we allow the devil to toy with our thoughts,
he'll influence our actions. "What you think about you bring
about," it's been said. Allow sin and negativity to spin through
your mind, and you'll live life as a puppet to Satan's whims.
This is why Paul instructs that we keep our minds fixed on

the goodness of God—on whatever is true, honorable, just, pure, pleasing, commendable, excellent, and worthy of praise (Phil. 4:8). These are salvation thoughts that protect us from the swing of Satan's sword, and they continue to produce victory in our lives.

There's one final article of the uniform to explore—the sword of the Spirit. It's a piece unlike all the others, because it's offensive rather than defensive, and it works to repel the enemy. I believe Paul lists it last because it puts all of the other pieces of armor into action. Let's move on to the next chapter and explore this weapon in greater detail.

Chapter 11

SHUT UP, DEVIL!

CREATION IS ESTABLISHED UPON THE POWER OF God's spoken word. This truth is contained within the very definition of the word we most commonly use to describe the cosmos. Consider the meaning of *universe*. It's the combination of two words: *uni*, which represents "one," and *verse*, which denotes a "spoken sentence." I smirk every time I hear a scientist lecture about "the universe that we live in," because he or she is actually affirming a significant truth from Scripture: you and I live inside of "one spoken sentence."

It's astonishing to think about the life-giving force of God's Word. He never lifted a finger, programmed one line of code, spent a single day in a laboratory, or made any blueprints to design the creation. He simply spoke one sentence, "Let there be...," and galaxies, stars, and planets all flung into position and instantly started doing their things. Every day the universe is upheld, and everything in it goes about their faithful dance all because God spoke just a few words so long ago. (See Hebrews 1:3.)

Since then God has spoken countless more words that contain the same life-giving power as the ones with which

He established creation. He's collected these words within a single book that we know as the Bible. This Bible has been esteemed as the "Word of God" for thousands of years. It's the world's number-one best-selling book, and according to the United Bible Societies, the complete Bible has been translated into more than four hundred fifty languages and the New Testament into more than twelve hundred languages.[1] The success of the Bible shouldn't be surprising to anyone; God would never let it falter. He considers His Word so important that He has equated it with His name.

> For you have exalted your name and your word above everything.
> —PSALM 138:2

In the last chapter we saw that Jesus's name represents ultimate victory. When His name is declared, all of creation must respect and obey it. Here we see that God's Word has that same power.

As ones who have been given Christ's authority, our inheritance includes the full power of God's Word. In fact, this is the final piece of armor that Paul says we possess in Christ. He urged that we "take…the sword of the Spirit, which is the Word of God" (Eph. 6:17) and use it during spiritual attack. "It's living and active," the writer to the Hebrews revealed, "sharper than any two-edged sword" (Heb. 4:12).

The Word as a sword is a potent metaphor. The soldier's sword is the only piece of armor that's offensive rather than just defensive. When not in use, it was carried in a sheath by his side or over his shoulder. But often it was taken out of its sheath and waved as a warning to the enemy to step back and retreat. With the sword the soldier could intimidate his adversary without ever leaving his position.

God gives us His Word as a sword to use in the same way

against Satan. But He doesn't mean for us to just lift up our Bibles and shake them around. That won't intimidate the enemy! Nor will just meditating upon it, as nice as that is. Notice that God didn't *think* creation into existence; He *spoke* it into existence. When it is spoken, the Word is activated as a weapon and maintains the same force that it did at Creation. Remember, the devil isn't all knowing, and so he can't read our thoughts. Like the soldier waving his sword, speaking the Word alerts Satan that you're armed and dangerous and won't be budged from your position in Christ.

Jesus's Model of Resisting Satan

Speaking Scripture aloud against the devil isn't something I came up with. It's the model given to us directly from Jesus. In fact, it's how He resisted Satan during His own temptation.

See the scene: John the Baptist baptizes Jesus in the Jordan River. It's a marvelous sight. As Jesus rises out of the murky water, the sky suddenly opens and the Spirit of God comes down like a dove and rests upon Jesus with a great light. The voice of God rises above the chatter of the onlookers and captures their attention. "This is my Son, the Beloved, with whom I am well pleased," God affirms (Matt. 3:17).

This is the first time recorded in Scripture that God declares an identity directly upon Jesus. He identified Him as His Son and that He was well pleased with Him. With this word Jesus would begin His earthly ministry and carry Himself with the confidence and authority of what His Father had spoken over Him.

But as many of us know all too well, a profound experience with God never lasts long without being tried. We have to be tested in order to know if we truly stand upon what we believe. Perhaps I neglected to mention that the attack that influenced this book happened just one day after I filmed a two-part series about spiritual warfare. I don't think this was a coincidence, but a test to see if I really believed what I preached. When you have a dramatic encounter with God or you believe you've heard from Him, don't be alarmed when you suddenly come against obstacles and voices that question everything.

This is what happened to Jesus. After His encounter with God He was immediately taken into the wilderness to be tempted (Matt. 4:1). Satan employed his usual tactics to try to steal Jesus's identity and authority. After a forty-day fast in the wilderness, Jesus was famished. He was at His weakest point, and in weakness is always the opportune time for Satan to pounce. Three times the devil found his way into Jesus's ear. I can almost envision the scene. I see Satan nestled in closely, invading Jesus's personal space. His breath tingles upon the tiny hairs of Jesus's ear lobes.

"If you are the Son of God," Satan instigates, "command these stones to become loaves of bread" (v. 3).

The devil questions what God had just declared. "Are You really the Son of God?" he implores. "Is that really what God said? Because if You are, then You should be able to turn stones into bread." It's a question meant to shake the foundation of Jesus's identity. Isn't this what you and I have heard ring through our minds too? "Are you really a Christian? Because if you are, you wouldn't have made that mistake," he accuses.

I want you to pay close attention to how Jesus handles Satan's whisper. Notice that He doesn't yell and scream, as if His volume would make any difference. Nor does He walk away, head held low in despair, and run to His disciples for prayer because "the devil's been lying to me." No, without even moving from His position, He calmly opens His mouth and confidently speaks.

It is written, "One does not live by bread alone, but by every word that comes from the mouth of God."

—MATTHEW 4:4,
emphasis added

It's critical to notice what Jesus spoke. "*It is written,*" He declared. He used Scripture—the truth of God—to counter Satan's lie.

The devil tries it again. He brings Jesus to the holy city, and this time he places Him at the "pinnacle of the temple," which is the highest point. According to scholars, this point was at least 450 feet above the ground. Anyone who jumped off would have faced certain death. Satan knows what he's doing by bringing Jesus to this high point. He makes his lie more potent by combining it with fear.

"If you are the Son of God," he again probes, "throw yourself down; for it is written, 'He will command his angels concerning you'" (v. 6).

"Again *it is written,*" Jesus counters without a flinch. "'Do not put the Lord your God to the test'" (v. 7, emphasis added).

Satan makes one final effort to undermine Jesus's identity. But this time it's a bit more disguised. From a high mountain the devil gives Jesus a panoramic view of all the kingdoms within sight. "All these I will give you, if you will fall down and worship me," Satan offers (v. 9).

Certainly the devil knows there's nothing he can actually offer Jesus, who owns everything anyway. But this is his subtle undermining. With his offer he covertly attempts to convince Jesus that He doesn't have what He actually has.

Doesn't the devil try the same in our lives? If he can't convince you that you aren't something that you are, he'll try to convince you that you don't have something you actually have. Let that sink in for a moment. This is why so much of the church experiences such heights of spiritual conflict today. Somehow Satan has undermined everything we've been given in Christ: forgiveness, righteousness, power, and authority. If we don't believe or know that we have these things, then Satan maintains dominance in our lives.

But Jesus won't have it; He won't concede dominion to the devil. "Away with you, Satan!" He commands. "For *it is written,* 'Worship the Lord your God, and serve only him'" (Matt. 4:10, emphasis added). In other words, *"Shut up, devil!"* With this demand Satan flees.

I want you to notice that in this story Jesus embodies each piece of the armor that we began to review in the last chapter. First, the truth of God is in Him so much that He can quickly counter Satan with it. His righteousness is never shaken, but rather He maintains confidence in His God-declared identity. This keeps Him calm, in control, and at peace throughout Satan's attack. Finally, with faith in God's Word, He speaks it aloud against Satan, after which Satan's voice is silenced and he retreats.

Clothed in Christ, we possess the authority of the Word of God so that we can resist the devil in the same way that Jesus did.

How to Apply the Word to Your Life Today

Certainly our victory was won at the cross, but it must be lived out every day. Inevitably the devil will come to question what God declared. As we've seen, he did it with Adam and Eve, Job, and even Jesus. The truth of God, found in His Word, is the only thing that consistently counters the feelings, lies, and accusations of Satan. So when he returns, we must be prepared to confront him with truth and send him on his way.

Speaking the Word of God has been absolutely crucial to lasting victory well after I ripped up my record of wrongs and experienced God declaring, "It is finished!" It's the key to keeping my mind focused on Christ and dead to the influences of Satan. Allow me to give you a practical pattern of how to apply this in your life today.

Find a relevant scripture.

Obviously the point is not to speak just any scripture, but one that's relevant to whatever situation you face. Notice that Jesus countered with a word directly related to the specific temptation Satan launched. For example, when the devil asked Him to prove Himself by turning stones in to bread, Jesus retorted with a scripture related to bread.

That's what I do. I know that God's Word has *everything* covered. Depression. Health. Jealousy. Laziness. Lust. Stress. You name it. There's not a condition or feeling known to man that God's Word doesn't offer some truth by which it may be overcome. So when Satan drops by with his whispers, I search for scriptures relevant to whatever lies I hear, emotions I feel, or situations in which I find myself.

Personalize the scripture.

When I locate a related verse, I often write it down on a notecard or enter it into my smartphone in a personalized way that's easy for me to speak aloud. This is key. The goal is to identify with the scripture so that it influences your identity. You must own what God says about you! To do this, I often add the word *I* in front of the verse and change the pronouns to first person. Here are some examples using several common issues that you might face.

Anxiety	"I don't worry about anything. Instead I seek the kingdom of God and His righteousness, and I trust that all of my needs will be met." (See Matthew 6:31–33.)
Depression	"God has turned my sadness into joyful dancing. He comforts me. I no longer mourn but sing praises and give thanks to God!" (See Psalm 30:11–12.)
Guilt	"I'm in Christ, and therefore I'm a new creation. My record of wrongs is erased, and I'm no longer defined by my past or mistakes, but I have a fresh start." (See 2 Corinthians 5:17.)
Insecurity	"I'm confident that God will be faithful to complete the good work that He began in me." (See Philippians 1:6.)
Temptation	"I submit myself to God. I resist the devil, and he must flee from me. I draw near to God, and He draws near to me." (See James 4:7–8.)

Speak and repeat.

You probably just read through those in your mind. But I want you to try this out for yourself. Reread these five personalized scriptures aloud, and as you do, imagine that you're countering Satan's whispers. When I do this, I sometimes see Satan's lie hovering above me in the air, but then it's struck down by the Word of God before it's able to touch me.

Be sure to stay persistent. Jesus responded to Satan three times before he finally fled. Keep your scriptures handy so that you can speak them aloud as often as you need. Be encouraged; the Bible promises that if you resist the devil, he *will* flee from you (James 4:7).

The Benefits of Speaking the Word

Isaiah says that the Word that comes out of God's mouth always accomplishes the purpose for which it was sent.

> For as the rain and the snow come down from heaven, and do not return there until they have watered the earth, making it bring forth and sprout, giving seed to the sower and bread to the eater, so shall my word be that goes out from my mouth; it shall not return to me empty, but it shall accomplish that which I purpose, and succeed in the thing for which I sent it.
>
> —ISAIAH 55:10–11

I believe that when the Word of God is spoken through the mouths of those in Christ, it contains the same power as if God has spoken it Himself. The words must maintain the authority of God, otherwise they couldn't accomplish anything. These are *His* words, not ours, after all. Have faith that when you speak the Word, it will always succeed, and over time you'll see its fruit in your life. Here are some of the benefits you should expect.

Speaking Scripture renews the mind.

Paul urged us not to behave according to the world, with its negativity, sinful habits, and misplaced desires. To live victoriously, our minds must be radically changed.

> Do not be conformed to this world, but be transformed by the renewing of your minds, so that you may discern what is the will of God—what is good and acceptable and perfect.
>
> —ROMANS 12:2

Part of our inheritance is the mind of Christ (1 Cor. 2:16). In fact, this is something that you should speak: "I have the mind of Christ." It's important to the resurrected life because the mind of Christ believes the truth of God over the hauntings of the past and the lies of Satan; it has unwavering faith in God's goodness.

This unwavering faith doesn't simply happen overnight, though. The transformation takes place over time through *hearing* the Word of God.

> So faith comes from what is heard, and what is heard comes through the word of Christ.
>
> —ROMANS 10:17

The spoken Word is powerful. Countless lives have been changed throughout the ages because the Word has been heard through sermons or Bible readings. But the Word is especially poignant when it comes out of our own mouths because we believe what we tell ourselves. Psychologists and motivational speakers have claimed this for years. You and I put more faith in what we hear ourselves say than what we hear others say.

Someone can tell you many times that you're beautiful or handsome. But it will never have a lasting effect until you genuinely say it yourself. If you want to have faith that you're forgiven, made worthy, or free from fear, speak it according to Scripture! Your mind will begin to believe what it hears, and eventually your entire life will reflect what you believe. When you speak the Word, that same power that gave life to the universe will give new life to you.

Please don't misunderstand this as New Age, "positive thinking" doctrine. We don't pump up ourselves with a bunch of "I can" self-talk, but rather we speak according to Christ's victory. "I can/I am *in Christ*" is our confession. The key to renewal of the mind is to get your confidence off of you and onto Christ. This only happens by speaking who you are and what you have *in Him*.

Speaking Scripture makes the devil flee.

I live in a gated, "no soliciting" apartment community where I rarely receive unannounced visitors. But on a cold night around eight fifteen there came a knock at my door. Besides the unusual timing, I had just come in from outside and saw no one around me. The knock came barely ten seconds after I locked the door behind me, so it almost seemed as if I was being watched. Still, I thought maybe someone needed help, so I cautiously answered.

On the other side stood a college-aged boy, rather disheveled, and obviously one of the more underprivileged of society. He began with a scripted spiel about how I could help him win a bunch of money. He barely made eye contact, but rather peered over my shoulder and into my living room.

I knew where it was headed. It's a known scam that you can Google. A seemingly low-income student is sent to your door to play on your emotions so that you write a check for some magazine subscriptions that you never actually receive. If you pass on the offer, he or she then asks for a drink or a snack, hoping to get quick access to your house to swipe something while your back is turned. A few years ago I'd fallen victim to this same trick, but this time I knew the truth, so I shut it down, and the boy swiftly went on his way.

This is precisely what happened when Jesus countered Satan's lies. The father of lies has no power when the truth of the Father is present. So when Jesus responded by saying, "It is written," the truth of God's Word exposed Satan's fraud, and he had to retreat.

When Satan unexpectedly knocks on your door to sell you his lies, immediately answer with truth. Two things happen when you respond with the Word. First, you activate that spiritual sword to pierce and cancel those lies and temptations before they affect your thoughts or behavior. Second, you remind Satan of his defeat. God's Word gives him a poignant flashback of everything he suffered at the cross.

The same spoken Word that gave humankind dominion

over the devil will keep Satan under your feet. Armed with the sword of the Spirit, Satan is a defeated foe with no leverage to attack. With this he quickly scampers away to move on to his next unsuspecting victim.

Speaking Scripture keeps Satan silenced.

We said that the Roman soldier would often wave his sword at the enemy as a word of warning to back off and retreat. Speaking Scripture aloud works in this same way. It's an offensive weapon because it has the power to keep Satan at a distance.

Of course, to be effective, the weapon has to be consistently used in this way. I find that just as soon as I stop speaking the Word, my focus wanes from Christ and more easily returns to my flesh. This gives Satan access to sneak up from behind and make me his victim again.

If you don't want to live under attack, you need to stay on the attack. The best way to stay on the attack is to make a habit of speaking Scripture as often as you can. I've worked to make this an essential practice throughout my day. I do my best to ensure that personalized Scriptures are with me at all times, and like preventative medicine, I speak them aloud even when I feel great and am not under any particular attack.

A habit of speaking Scripture aloud keeps your mind renewed and confident in Christ. Therefore you aren't as susceptible to the things that try to shake you. But the same Word that set the boundaries of earth and sky, land and ocean, will also keep Satan at bay in your life. The sword of the Spirit signals, "Stay back, devil! I'm armed with the truth of God."

Talk Back to the Devil!

In chapter 5 I discussed Martin Luther's torturous struggle with condemnation. The devil kept a cloud of accusations over him so much that he felt he had to beat himself. But as we learned, Luther finally received a revelation of the cross as the final, once-and-for-all payment of sin. This set Luther free from his torment and gave him a new boldness. He no longer put up with Satan's voice, but instead he talked back to the devil using the force of God's Word. Luther shared how he countered Satan:

> So when the devil throws your sins in your face and declares that you deserve death and hell, tell him this: "I admit that I deserve death and hell, what of it? For I know One who suffered and made satisfaction on my behalf. His name is Jesus Christ, Son of God, and where He is there I shall be also!"[2]

As I've already said, Satan will return from time to time in attempts to question you. He might even bring you to an edge, as he did to Jesus, and add fear to his whispers. But now you possess a powerful weapon that Satan must obey, so you don't have to become his victim ever again.

When the devil brings you to the edge of your bank account, your marriage, or even your job, and whispers, "What if?", counter him with God's Word. When he claims that you don't have what you really have—that you're unworthy, that your sins are too big to be forgiven, or that your situation is hopeless—do as Jesus did, as Luther did, and as I have learned to do, and talk back to him. I exclaim, "Shut up, devil!" and so can you.

Say it with me now, *"Shut up, devil!"*

◊ *I don't preach out of my own perfection but out of the perfection that covers me in Christ!*

◊ *God will use me because He declares me good enough!*

⋄ *My past doesn't define me; I'm made new in Christ!*

⋄ *Temptations won't influence me; I'm dead to sin!*

⋄ *Fear won't hold me back; I'm free and bold!*

⋄ *These symptoms don't scare me; I'm healed in Jesus's name!*

Doesn't it feel great to talk back to the devil?

Chapter 12

THE VOICE OF TRUTH

ACH OF US IS BORN INTO THIS WORLD LIKE A NEW page in the journal of life. For just a few short minutes we're blank and unmarked, with no words yet written between the evenly ruled lines on our sheets. We lay there helplessly open to whatever or whoever comes along to write, draw, scribble, or even color upon our individual pages.

Within minutes or hours of birth someone comes along to give headings to our lives. Printing boldly across the tops of our pages, they define each of us with a name. Perhaps after a loved one, a Bible character, a song, or even a special place, our parents select a name that means something, if only to them. Our first names give the very first definition of who we are. We'll answer to it for the rest of our lives. Our last names aren't as negotiable, but they represent *whose* we are. And like it or not, they carry much of the esteem and baggage of those who share these last names in the pages before our own. We have no say in any of this. The unique identities with which we each enter the world were chosen for us.

Every day thereafter we experience a variety of new things—discouragements and disappointments, encouragements and successes. Many of these, at least early on, are also not results of our own choices, but they are of someone else's words or actions. These experiences are nonetheless recorded onto our pages, which by now appear like identity profiles. How we enter our adult lives, whether insecure or confident, is often reflective of all of this graffiti.

Based upon experiences from the past, I entered adulthood with an identity of insecurity and rejection. I explained in chapter 3 about my extreme shyness throughout my elementary years and how it caused me to be an outcast in school. My most developmental years were characterized by being misunderstood by those my same age. And when kids don't understand you, they tend to do so with cruelty.

I dreaded whenever teachers allowed us to pick partners for a class project. I'd inevitably sit alone and overhear the whispers of why or why not certain people, including me, should be chosen. I rarely experienced someone who wanted to be my partner, so instead I waited until everyone else was chosen. Whoever was left was mine by default. PE class was especially difficult because at least a couple times a week I'd hear someone say some version of, "No, don't choose him; he's a wimp."

I remember being extremely shamed when a classmate revealed to an older cousin of mine, "Kyle doesn't have any friends." In that moment I just wanted to hide under a rock. I felt humiliated like some dirty secret had been exposed, and now my family knew the truth.

The words spoken about me in my youth were like bullet points under the name on my page; they defined who "Kyle Winkler" was. "I *am* a person that no one wants to choose. I *am* a wimp. I *am* a reject," I came to believe.

This identity was my reality, so I thought, and was the lens through which I perceived many situations in my adult life. In high school, and somewhat through college, I was often a friend to the friendless—not out of compassion, but because I figured if I pursued friendship with someone other than those who were desperate for companionship, I'd only be rejected. "Why put myself through more pain?" I reasoned. Instead I waited and waited for whoever might choose me.

Later, when I was involved in the political world, I dreaded the all-too common socials where mingling was essential. I'd enter the room with a lump in my throat and butterflies in my stomach. If I saw people in the corner laughing, I just figured they must have been laughing at me. This often paralyzed me from approaching anyone. It was a horrible way to live. For too many years I was shackled by an identity based upon things that I didn't choose.

Satan's Script

As I said, I came to accept my identity as the things that had been said about me. "I am my feelings. I am my past. This is the way it's always been; this is how it will always be," I thought. The trap in all of this is that it becomes an endless cycle—a script by which we live our lives. In many situations I'd end up being rejected only because I expected to be rejected.

An abuse victim might follow her script like this: "I was abused by men all of my life, so therefore I will always keep my distance from men and never treat any man kindly. I *am* a victim and always will be." A former addict might use his script to remain hopeless: "People know me for my mistakes. I *am* just a junkie." Those who struggle with depression, for example, tend to think they are their feelings: "I'm always sad. I always feel discouraged and never good enough. I *am* depressed." To think like this is extremely crippling because you often rise only to the level of who you believe you are.

Satan, of course, adds his lies to the rhapsody of words that attempt to define us. "You're a sinner," he accuses. "*God can't use sinners!*" His goal is to get you to identify with your sin so that you don't identify with Christ, and thus you have no victory.

How often have you heard a well-meaning Christian say, "I'm just a sinner saved by grace"? With their heads held low, they confess it almost pathetically. It might as well end with, "Now I'll just go eat some worms!"

Perhaps no statement incites a righteous fury in me more than this one. It's incredibly dangerous because it affects your behavior. What do sinners do? They sin! As soon as you accept this identity, you'll predictably continue in the cycle, bound by condemnation, which is exactly what Satan wants.

It's also perhaps one of the subtlest lies because it sounds spiritual and so humble. We think that it's holy to call ourselves sinners because it keeps us from being prideful. But really, it's verbal abuse! It's no different from the physical floggings that Martin Luther used to endure in order to pay for his sin. Referring to yourself as a sinner won't bring you any more forgiveness; it will only wound your soul and keep you enslaved to this identity.

Many seem to believe that humility requires a negative opinion of yourself, which isn't true. The biblical definition is much more balanced:

> **humility**—the personal quality of being free from arrogance and pride and having an accurate estimate of one's worth[1]

To say that you're "saved by grace" is honest. It recognizes that you were rescued from a life of darkness. But to claim that you're still a sinner denies the grace that saved you. It maintains an identity with the past from which Christ came to redeem and set you free. It's actually more arrogant than humble because it minimizes the power of Christ's cross. I'm sure most who say this don't think about it in this way, but claiming to remain a sinner actually says to Jesus, "Your wounds, your blood, your death weren't worth enough."

"But we still sin," people argue. Of course we do! But just as bouts of sadness don't define you as depressed, nor a past of rejection define you as a reject, a believer who occasionally sins isn't defined as a "sinner." *Sinner* is not his or her identity. Don't accept this script! Your worth is found in Christ, who is righteous and holy. It's therefore completely humble and accurate to identify yourself as righteous and holy *in Him*.

God-Given Identities

Throughout the Bible God often changed the names of those who genuinely encountered Him. He did this in order to give that person a new identity. In each case the new identity went against all common sense and the situation that the person was currently in. God, who sees the end from the beginning, gave each prophetically. "This is how *I* see you," He said. "And how I see you is what you are to base your future upon." Let's take a look at a few of these.

Abram to Abraham

Abram, whose name meant "the father is exalted," was chosen for a monumental destiny. His descendants were to be so numerous and his lineage so great that they would bless the entire earth (Gen. 12:1–3). "Look toward the heaven and count the stars, if you are able to count them" God instructed him. "So shall your descendants be" (Gen. 15:5).

But when God called him to take a faith step toward His destiny, it all seemed impossible because his wife, Sarai, was barren. How could he have even one descendant, much less as many as the stars in the sky?

But God didn't see Abram and Sarai in their current

situations. When it came time to bless them with children, God changed their identities. He said to Abram: "You shall be the ancestor of a multitude of nations. No longer shall your name be Abram, but your name shall be Abraham; for I have made you the ancestor of a multitude of nations" (Gen. 17:4–5). The Lord continued, "As for Sarai your wife, you shall not call her Sarai, but Sarah shall be her name. I will bless her, and moreover I will give you a son by her. I will bless her, and she shall give rise to nations; kings of peoples shall come from her" (Gen. 17:15–16).

Abram's—now Abraham's—response to God wasn't anything particularly spiritual. In fact, he responded in much the same way you or I might. He laughed. "There's no way," he basically conceded. It was hopeless enough that Sarah was barren, but by this time she was also well beyond her childbearing years. But still God had changed their names to "father" and "mother of nations," and with it He changed their destinies.

Notice that God gave Abraham and Sarah their new identities before they saw even a glimmer of what was promised. We know this was tough for Abraham to comprehend. On several occasions God had to remind him of His word. Still, God wasn't moved by their feelings or their present circumstances. "Despite what you see, hear, and feel, this is who you are," He more or less assured. Of course, God was faithful to bring it to pass, and with their son, Isaac, Abraham and Sarah eventually saw the realization of what God had determined long before.

Jacob to Israel

The birth of Isaac was the beginning of the fulfillment of God's promise. Eventually Isaac and his wife, Rebekah, were blessed with twins. While the babies were still in the womb, God determined their identities. "Two nations are in your womb," He revealed, "and two peoples born of you shall be divided; the one shall be stronger than the other, the elder shall serve the younger" (Gen. 25:23). At the moment of conception God chose Jacob, the younger of the twins, to lead the nation that would be the blessing to the earth that He had promised Abraham.

But Jacob means "supplanter," or in other words, "one who deceives." This is a fitting description of one whose life was characterized by employing deception to achieve his goals. His father in his old age sought to give the customary blessing to the oldest son, Esau. But Jacob wanted the blessing for himself. And so he disguised himself as Esau and tricked his nearly blind father into giving it to him (Gen. 27:1–29.).

Although masterfully deceptive, Jacob was a coward and didn't appear to be the stronger of the two. When Esau recognized what Jacob had done, he was infuriated and plotted to kill him. In fear Jacob fled. For years to come he'd continue this habit, fleeing from one place to the next, and using deception to cover deception (Gen. 32:13–21).

But as we all know, you can't run from problems forever. Eventually Jacob received word that Esau was coming to meet him. Afraid of what his brother might do, he devised a plan to split his camp into two and sent them on ahead so that he was left alone for a night. In this moment Jacob feared that all of his deception had finally caught up to him. Perhaps he'd come to the lowest point in his life, which many of us know is a ripe place to encounter God.

In his lonely night of despair he happened upon a man with whom he wrestled until daybreak. Jacob put up a good fight, but the man struck one final blow and wounded his hip. This was possibly the first time Jacob showed the strength that was prophesied of him. He persisted in this grapple until the man spoke a blessing over him. "What's your name?" the man inquired. "Jacob," he answered.

Jacob wrestled with no mere man, though. He had encountered God Himself that night. I believe that God's question regarding Jacob's name was actually to get Jacob to confess his identity before Him. "Who are you?" God asked. "I am one who deceives," Jacob humbly responded. With this admission Jacob was ready to have his old identity exchanged for a new one. "You shall no longer be called Jacob, but Israel," God declared, "for you have striven with God and with humans, and have prevailed" (Gen 32:28).

In a single encounter God transformed Jacob from "the one who deceives" to Israel, which means "the one who prevails with God." Even after this encounter Jacob didn't always feel or appear as one who prevails. Yet God's order made it official in the heavenlies and set the course for his destiny. Israel would indeed become a strong nation and a blessing to the entire earth. It would be the nation through which Jesus would enter the world.

Simon to Peter

For most of his life Peter was known as Simon. This was a common name in those days, which was fitting of who he was—just a regular ol' guy from a small fishing town. But personally selected by Christ as an apostle, this common man was destined for a role no others in history could claim.

Literally, *Simon* means "listener," which also represented him well. In the early days of his time with Christ I imagine he meticulously observed everything about the man he followed so that he knew, without any doubt, who Jesus was. Simon was ready when Jesus asked His apostles, "Who do you say that I am?" He responded without hesitation: "You are the Messiah, the Son of the living God" (Matt. 16:16). With this he found favor in Jesus's eyes. "Blessed are you, Simon son of Jonah!" Jesus exclaimed. In this moment his name was changed to reveal his destiny. "And I tell you, you are Peter," Jesus asserted, "and on this rock I will build my church, and the gates of Hades will not prevail against it" (vv. 17–18).

In an instant Simon became Peter. Scholars note that Peter, which means "rock," wasn't used as a personal name in those days. It was as rare as naming someone "Concrete" is today. And though Peter's faith that day may have seemed particularly solid and "rock-like," it didn't always remain that way. From time to time Peter experienced some rather weak moments. He fell asleep in the garden while Jesus prayed (Mark 14:37), and most famously, he denied Jesus three times in order to protect his reputation (Matt. 26:69–75).

Peter's weaknesses, however, didn't change the fact that Jesus declared him to be the rock upon which His church would be founded. He would eventually rise to the level of his newfound identity. On the Day of Pentecost he preached a bold message of repentance and saw nearly three thousand people added to the faith (Acts 2:41). Though he had his moments, this common man became a world changer, and his unflinching faith was the foundation upon which many came to Christianity.

Your New Identity

In each story above the new identity was given through an encounter with God. It was never achieved through merit, but it was received, and often by the most unlikely person. When God declared Abraham as "father of many nations," this is who he was although his current circumstances didn't reflect it. In Jacob's wrestling match with God, he confessed his born identity, and despite his past, he was then regarded as a victor. Though Peter didn't always remain solid, God chose him as a "rock" and never reconsidered.

Like Abraham, Israel, and Peter, God has a calling upon

your life too. He's prepared for you to be a member of His family—a child of God.

> We know that all things work together for good for those who love God, who are called according to his purpose. For those whom he foreknew he also pre-destined to be conformed to the image of his Son, in order that he might be the firstborn within a large family. And those whom he predestined he also called; and those whom he called he also justified; and those whom he justified he also glorified.
> —ROMANS 8:28–30

Regardless of your past or present circumstances, God is committed to giving you His name and bringing you into His family. In an encounter with Jesus at the cross, we confess our former identities and we lay them there. In this moment all the words that filled our pages and that once defined us—our records of wrongs—are erased. These false identities are cruci-fied at the cross, where their power is canceled. We get a brand-new start.

> This means that anyone who belongs to Christ has become a new person. The old life is gone; a new life has begun!
> —2 CORINTHIANS 5:17, NLT

This is remarkable! We are completely new in Christ. In our newness, however, God doesn't then leave us without an iden-tity. We don't begin again as a blank page, helplessly open to whoever comes along to scribble on it. No, we're transformed into the image of Jesus. As we learned in the last chapter, we put on the identity of Christ, and so we're defined by every-thing that He is.

Throughout the book we've touched on some of these

things. But I want to use the second half of this chapter to explore the foundations of your new identity in Christ more fully. I encourage you to bookmark this page and use it as a place to quickly return to when you need the encouragement of God's truth.

God chose you.

There's a prevailing lie that's infiltrated much of the culture. The propaganda that you and I are products of some primordial soup that randomly formed together to create life is spread throughout our classrooms and television programs. "There's no purpose or reason for existence," is what's implied. "We're all just accidents of evolution." This notion of purposelessness is further bolstered by the epidemic of fatherlessness. Many today are raised in homes of an absent parent. The lines on their pages are filled with feelings of being unwanted or abandoned, which they often relate to their heavenly Father. Accordingly many believe they're meaningless to God or that He's forgotten about them too.

It may be true that your parents were surprised by your arrival, but you are no surprise to God. God's words to the prophet Jeremiah reveal that He is the one who forms us in the womb and knows each of us before we're born.

> Before I formed you in the womb I knew you, and before you were born I consecrated you.
> —JEREMIAH 1:5

The truth is that God had you in mind and created you before your parents ever conceived you. Like a potter's hand to clay, God crafted you with great care, from the inside out (Ps. 139:13). He didn't overlook a single detail. Your eye color, the shape of your nose, the color of your skin—none of it was an afterthought, but it was all meticulously chosen by your heavenly Father. Like David, you should exclaim, "I am fearfully and wonderfully made" (v. 14)!

Let me also let you in on a little secret. *God knows you better than you know yourself.* David revealed just how extensive God's knowledge is of us.

> You know when I sit down and when I rise up; you discern my thoughts from far away. You search out my path and my lying down, and are acquainted with all my ways. Even before a word is on my tongue, O LORD, you know it completely.
> —PSALM 139:2–4

Did it ever dawn on you that nothing ever dawns on God? In whatever place you sit right now—physically and emotionally—God is not surprised. Think about that. He knows all of your ways, thoughts, and words; He knew what He was getting before He formed you. Despite the good, the bad, and the ugly, God still chose to bring you into existence with the hope that you would one day enter His family.

> Long, long ago he decided to adopt us into his family through Jesus Christ. (What pleasure he took in planning this!)
> —EPHESIANS 1:5, THE MESSAGE

God chose to include your page in His book, regardless of the mess you made of it. Here's how I envision His thoughts for me before I was formed (put your name in the place of mine as you are reading this): "I know Kyle will mess up more times than not. But I'm taking a chance on him to accept My Son, Jesus, and enter into My family. I'm not afraid of his past—I have a plan to erase that. A relationship with Kyle is worth the price I have to pay for it."

You are not an accident, nor are you unwanted. Regardless of the way you entered this world or what's happened since you've been here, you are God's desire. Build your confidence upon this profound three-word truth and speak it: "God chose me!"

God is not mad at you.

I remember hearing as a child, "Don't do that, or God will get you back!" The image I had of God was of a distant being that peered down from heaven, who stood hands crossed and scowling, waiting to zap whoever upset Him. This naturally formed a fear in me toward God. It wasn't the holy fear of the Lord that inspires awe and wonder, but it was the fear that keeps you away from someone.

Even as an adult I hear this notion implied in various ways throughout the culture. The latest natural disaster always incites speculation that God is angry. He's also an easy target for the cause of sickness and disease. It's implied that these are all the works of God trying to get our attention.

It's a slick deception of the devil to ascribe his works to God. It removes him from the limelight and instead makes God out to be the bad guy. In doing this, he effectively does two things: (1) he keeps people in misery because they believe their suffering is God's will, and (2) he keeps people hidden from God, like Adam and Eve, living in guilt and shame.

If Satan can convince you that God is mad at you, you won't expect God's goodness, but you'll expect misery instead. But those who know God's love have confidence in His goodness. This was the key to David's strength to endure battle and overcome his enemies. "Now my head is lifted up above my enemies all around me," he said while his adversaries breathed down his back (Ps. 27:6). David understood God's profound love for him so much that he expected it to see him through. "I believe I shall see the goodness of the LORD in the land of the living," he boasted in faith (v. 13).

Ultimately the devil wants you to take your eyes off of the cross. If you believe that God consistently desires to punish you for everything you do wrong, then you have a shallow view of Calvary. The enormity of the cross is that Jesus satisfied the punishment for sin with the bloodiest massacre in history. Here, wave after wave of God's wrath poured down upon Him. He drank the cup of God's wrath so that you and I don't have to. There's no greater love.

> No one has greater love than this, to lay down one's life for one's friends.
>
> —JOHN 15:13

Jesus considers you His friend, and He chose to lay down His life for you. And get this: He didn't choose to do it after you were all fixed and perfect (as if that's ever possible!). No, Jesus saw you in your worst condition and in your darkest places, and He still chose to die for you.

> But God proves his love for us in that while we still were sinners Christ died for us.
>
> —ROMANS 5:8

The magnitude of God's love is astonishing. Only someone so infatuated could be so forgiving. Only someone so madly in love would go to the extreme of death to prove it. And that's the picture of Jesus toward you. God is not trying to "get you back" or inflict pain and suffering upon you. Punishment was taken care of at the cross. He's not mad at you, but He's mad about you!

The declaration that "God loves me" may be your greatest weapon in spiritual warfare. It silences Satan's lies with confidence in God's goodness. God's love links you in an impenetrable bond with Him that no devil in hell can separate (Rom. 8:38–39).

God will use you.

The result of Satan's whispers into my ear was the fear that "God can't use me." As we've seen throughout the book, this is ultimately the place that his accusations are intended to lead. Completely overcome with guilt and shame, Judas came to this place, and it killed him. In the least, the idea that God can't use you will silence your voice and kill your destiny in Christ.

The Bible likens you and me to jars of clay. It's a humbling metaphor, actually, because jars of clay are brittle and fragile. If dropped, they instantly shatter into pieces. Upon close inspection you'll notice inconsistencies, flaws, chips, cracks, and imperfections. A jar of clay isn't something of major value on its own, but rather it's just ordinary at best.

Now, take your mind off of being just a common ol' jar of clay, and see your value in what God has placed inside of you.

> But we have this *treasure* in clay jars, so that it may be made clear that this extraordinary power belongs to God and does not come from us.
> —2 CORINTHIANS 4:7,
> emphasis added

The treasure that you and I contain is the glory of God! Why would God place His riches into something so fragile? Why would He give the best of Himself and put it into you and me? The answer is inconceivable: to demonstrate His power.

Let me explain. Naturally, I'm introverted. You won't see me as the social butterfly at the party or making much small talk in the elevator. Around large groups of strangers I tend to clam up. I used to beat myself up about this, as if my personality was something to be cast out. Then God calmed me down. "I gave you that personality so that My strength is seen in your weakness," He assured (2 Cor. 12:9). And that's precisely the case. Though I can sometimes seem "quiet," I'm quite the opposite when I preach. People find it very unexpected, in fact. From the platform, boldness arises in me that I can't take the credit for. There's no other choice but to say, "That's God!" And I'm completely OK with that.

Throughout Scripture God has a habit of using the most unlikely; He often takes nobodies and turns them into somebodies. Remember Abraham's story? He was just an old, brittle jar of clay, and his wife was a barren, empty one. But their weaknesses caused God no reconsideration. In fact, their weaknesses only glorified Him all the more. We marvel at their story not because a perfect couple achieved a typical feat, but because an unlikely couple experienced the impossible.

Consider the flaws of some of the other men and women of God in Scripture. Noah got drunk. Jacob was a deceiver. Moses had a stutter. Rahab was a prostitute. Jonah ran from God. Mary Magdalene was demon possessed. Peter denied Jesus three times. I could go on and on. The Bible is littered with heroes who, despite their pasts or shortcomings, were mightily used by God simply because they allowed Him to display His strength through their weaknesses.

Satan loves to point out your weaknesses in order to convince you that it's simply not possible for God to use you. Don't let the voice of "look what you've done," "you're too this" or "you're not enough of that" disqualify you. Know that your wounds, your past, and your weaknesses, when taken to the cross, are actually the things that are used powerfully in God's service and are the very things that silence Satan in your life. God has chosen you, He loves you, and even against all odds, He has a plan to use you.

On a blank sheet of paper write your full name. Think of it

as if you are being given a new page in life's journal, but this time you get to put the heading on it yourself. Then read this list of things that God says about you in His Word.

- ◊ I am created in God's image (Gen. 1:27).
- ◊ I am a child of God (John 1:12).
- ◊ I am a friend of God (John 15:15).
- ◊ I am loved by God (Rom. 5:8).
- ◊ I am a new creature (2 Cor. 5:17).
- ◊ I am righteous (2 Cor. 5:21).
- ◊ I am holy (Eph. 1:4).
- ◊ I am chosen by God (Eph. 1:5).
- ◊ I am accepted (Eph. 1:6).
- ◊ I am forgiven (Eph. 1:7).

Begin to see and think of yourself according to these things. Try to forget how you feel or whatever your circumstances are, but let the words of God define you. This was absolutely crucial to overcoming my past and the rejection that had defined me. I had to accept that my past, my feelings, and what others said about me were not my reality. The ultimate reality—what trumps everything else—is what God says. And He says that you and I are made new in Christ! Allow His Word, and nothing else, to be the voice of truth that defines your identity and determines your destiny.

Chapter 13

SPEAK UP!

CAROL WAS BORN INTO A HOUSEHOLD DEVOID OF love. Just one in a litter of children, and the product of an affair, she never felt particularly wanted. Her mom divided most of her time between all the siblings, so there wasn't much left to give Carol. She received even less from her father who, because of the circumstances of her birth, made her the victim of his resentment.

On many occasions Carol was awoken in the night to one of her parents' all-too-common drunken rages. She dodged dishes and beer bottles flying through the air from their knock-down-drag-out fights. Often these arguments pertained to her mom's adultery. "She's not mine," she'd hear her father sneer, obviously remarking about her.

Carol's dad could never forgive his wife for the mistake she'd made in her early twenties. Nor could he forgive Carol for *being* this mistake. Throughout her early years she paid a high price for her miserable existence with beatings and unspeakable kinds of abuse.

The words spoken about her and the experiences she suffered developed an identity of shame. "I am unloved; I am unwanted; I am an outcast; I am a victim," she believed. These feelings plagued her well into her early adult life.

Understandably, when Carol came of age and got the chance to leave, there was no looking back. She ran from that household as quickly as should could, and she did so in search of the love and acceptance she never felt at home.

Even if she was never noticed by anyone else, you can be sure that Satan studied her life. I'm certain he was convinced that Carol, with so many wounds, would be an easy target to get within his grips. So around the corner he lurked, and he lured her with his usual attractive but empty promises. Carol took the bait.

The next decade of her life was spent bound by his chains. She began a promiscuous, drug-laden life, and she found herself checked in and out of mental wards. She'd get pregnant and have an abortion, just to do it over again twice more.

Then at her lowest point the devil offered her something she'd always wanted—power. That is, his perverted version of power through witchcraft and the occult. Carol became fascinated with her newfound religion and opened herself up to many spirits, all promising wisdom and guidance.

But as many of us know, Satan's fun only lasts so long before his true intentions are made obvious. Every experience inched her down the road to her death. When the devil had her right where he wanted, the "wisdom" stopped and the whispers began. "You're useless. You haven't done one decent thing your entire life. Nobody loves you. Kill yourself," he taunted.

Carol's journey might be one that illustrates Satan's plan so completely...*if it ended here.* But it doesn't. In fact, the devastation of her early years makes her story all the more amazing.

Just before her life ended in death, it took a dramatic turn. Carol began to work at a bar, which happened to be the mission field of a sweet, unassuming Christian lady named Linda.

Immediately Carol became Linda's mission. Day after day Linda invited her to church and gently talked to her about Jesus. Linda was unrelenting at showing God's love, regardless of Carol's low-cut clothing and foul mouth.

Linda personifies the passionate pursuit God makes for His children. Through her He chased Carol into a bar—at the darkest time in her life—in order to bring her back from death and into new life.

Eventually Carol gave in to Linda's persistence and agreed to attend a special church meeting. Carol sat at the back of the church, anxiously waiting for it all to be over. But the end was just the beginning, because the preacher concluded at the cross. "The death of Jesus was horrific," he explained. "First, the soldiers ripped out His beard with their bare hands. They spit in His face and beat Him with whips, tearing His back to shreds."[1] He led the congregation to behold Jesus as a lamb and boasted in the blood of Christ as the means of complete forgiveness and oneness with God.

Carol was jittery and wanted to leave. In fact, she began to feel sick, and her mind raced with confusion. The evil inside of her went crazy. "You're a whore and a drug addict, and nobody wants you in this church," she heard play through her mind. The devil knew that his influence in her life was about to end, and so he fought with the last of his might to stop her. But when you become the focus of God's zealous pursuit, no devil can get in the way.

As the congregation passionately erupted into a song about the blood, Linda led Carol to front. People gawked as she stumbled down the aisle. Shouts exploded in her mind: "You're crazy!" Then the music stopped, and all attention turned toward her. Suddenly a gentle roar of prayer filled the air, and she melted to the floor.

"In this moment pictures of my past went off in my head.

One by one they flashed before my eyes," Carol recalls. It was the record of her wrongs and every emotion associated with all the junk from the past: rejection, sorrow, remorse, shame, and betrayal. Lying on the ground, she sobbed and sobbed until an indescribable peace overtook her. It was the voice of truth. "Carol, My name is Jesus Christ, and if you're looking for love, you found it. I love you just the way you are," He assured.

In this single encounter with Jesus Carol's identity was forever changed. For the first time in her life she felt pure love. No longer a reject or an outcast, "I *am* loved," she came to realize. Carol was delivered that day. The voices were forever silenced by Jesus's blood. His bruises healed her wounds. She walked out of that church with the resurrected life that God so furiously pursued her to give.

The One-Two Punch
Against the Devil

Carol could have taken her healing and went on to enjoy her new life in a respectable, quiet way. Nobody would have minded. In fact, many might understand if she wanted to remain discreet about the life she lived and the mistakes she made.

Though she was immediately healed of the effects of years of Satan's influences, there was more victory to be had. And it came when she opened her mouth. She knew that the story of her past contained the power to set others in similar situations free. And so rather than remain quiet, Carol determined to share her story. Since that time thousands have benefited from her openness.

Carol's story is a great example of everything we've discussed. But it's also a vivid illustration of what the Bible reveals is the one-two punch to keep Satan's accusations silenced in our lives.

For the accuser of our brothers and sisters has been thrown down to earth—the one who accuses them before our God day and night. And they have defeated him by the blood of the Lamb and by their testimony. And they did not love their lives so much that they were afraid to die.

—REVELATION 12:10–11, NLT

Satan's accusations are silenced by the blood *and* by our testimonies. A testimony is "proof or evidence that something exists or is true."[2] Your testimony is the evidence or proof of how you made it through your toughest circumstance. It's the evidence of how you overcame your past. For some, it's the evidence of how you're even still alive today. To put it simply, your testimony is your story, which includes the pain you've been through.

Evidence of Victory

We have all had experiences that have cut us to the core. Some of these things are our own faults; others aren't. Many of these moments in life have left us marked by visible or invisible signs of the past. We talked a lot about this throughout the book. Someone who once struggled with sexual sin may have had an inner feeling of shame. An abuse victim may have felt unloved. A former drug addict might exhibit needle scars. These moments and feelings may mark the beginning of our testimonies, but they aren't the end.

The wonder of the cross, as we now know, is its healing power. When sin and shame are nailed there, our old identities are crucified, and we put on the identity of Christ. This is the place where wounds become scars.

Scars are simply wounds that are healed. Because they're healed, they no longer carry the pain they once did. They are no longer haunting reminders of a shameful past, but they are evidences of healing and reminders of victory. We should never regret them or believe we have to hide them. Our scars tell our stories and have tremendous ability to give hope to those who see or hear of them.

Again, Jesus is our pinnacle example. We observed the horrendous wounds that He suffered because of the guilt and shame put upon Him at the cross. We beheld the pain He endured as He became our sin. None of the wounds He suffered were His fault.

Upon rising from the dead, Jesus could have appeared with a redeemed body that completely erased all signs of the past. He could have stepped out of the tomb completely perfect, and people would have marveled at His new body. But Jesus chose to do something much more powerful.

> Jesus came and stood among them and said, "Peace be with you." After he said this, he showed them his hands and his side.
> —JOHN 20:19–20

Jesus stood in that room with His disciples and revealed the marks of what He went through on the cross. He kept the scars from the things He had suffered as evidence that there stood a man who should be dead but is now alive. His scars are His testimony, and they tell His story. And for those who behold them, they are reminders of His victory.

The Benefits of Sharing Your Story

Jesus understood the tremendous power of what He had done, and He gave it to us as a model to follow. When He left His disciples that day, He said, "As the Father has sent me, so I send you" (John 20:21). And He commissions us in the same way. Forty days later, just before His ascension, He gave the church this final charge:

> But you will receive power when the Holy Spirit has come upon you; and you will be my witnesses in Jerusalem, in all Judea and Samaria, and to the ends of the earth.
>
> —ACTS 1:8

"Be my witnesses." These are Jesus's famous last words. Perhaps you expected something more profound. But there's no purpose more substantial than to be His witness.

We understand this more clearly when we define the word. A witness is simply one who experiences something and tells others about his or her experience. That's it! This is our ultimate mission! Jesus instructs us to encounter Him and talk about it. It's a charge to tell our stories—not just for the fun of it or to keep us busy, but because it's key to ongoing victory in our lives, and it releases His power in the lives of others. I believe the sharing of our stories is the final key to the resurrected life for each of us.

Let's explore this now.

Sharing your story connects you with others.

It was my first trip to India, and throughout the two-week stay I was slated to preach to various groups across the southern half of the country. The single greatest rule of communication is to know your audience so that you can speak according to their interests. I certainly broke this one. I didn't know the age groups, education levels, or even much about the culture of those to whom I would speak.

Most of what I had prepared was related to my testimony. In the days leading up to the first speaking engagement, I became very insecure. "Can these people relate to the things

I've gone through?" I wondered. "Are my first-world problems really even problems in a third world? Will the translation of my stories make any sense?"

Later that week, at a Bible school filled with young Indian men, I spoke passionately about the issues I faced as a child, the sins of my adult life, the accusations Satan launched at me, and the victory of the cross. I could see the men shaking their heads in agreement and hanging on to my every word, as if they'd experienced something similar. Though the message ended with the claps and "amens" that every preacher covets, I still wondered if it made any real impact upon these students.

Our driver that night happened to be one of the young men in the class. As I climbed in to the front seat, he patted my leg, looked me in the eye, and with his best broken English he said, "Your story is my story." He reiterated the same words to me several more times throughout the next two days. He didn't know enough English to be able to say anything more, but his persistent demeanor of gratitude said it all. Somehow, someway, he was able to relate with the things I had gone through, and it built a respect and connection between us. Throughout my time with him I was able to minister more effectively simply because our struggles linked us in a common bond.

Though I had a translator, I believe the Holy Spirit did most of the translation during that trip. And I learned a valuable lesson. As we tell our stories, the Holy Spirit transforms our words to relate to people whom we might even consider far beyond our own contexts.

Before I began to be this vulnerable, people tended to treat me as a super-spiritual personality who had it all together. Boy, did I have them fooled! The perception was that I was unapproachable and likely to judge a person's mistakes. Now that I reveal my scars through the testimony of my past, I'm humanized. Rather than "I can never be him," people often see themselves through my story and say, "I am him." Because they identify with the things I've gone through, people are much more interested in how I've gone through them.

I promise that you'll notice the same. As soon as you open your life to show your scars, you're brought to the level of struggling people. Only at that level do you have real opportunities to heal the brokenhearted.

Sharing your story raises you above the influence of your past.

Some believe that they're completely healed of their wounds and freed of their pasts, yet they're too embarrassed to speak about them. Those of us in ministry are especially susceptible to this. We're cautious about being too vulnerable because it might break the façade of a well-put-together minister. We fear we might lose some amount of authority or that people will treat us differently if they know the truth. I understand this, because I used to be there. But embarrassment about sharing your testimony is ultimately rooted in pride and only keeps you under the influence of your past, not above it.

Consider again what the Bible says is the winning combo by which we defeat the devil: the blood of the Lamb, the word of our testimony, "*and they did not love their lives so much that they were afraid to die*" (Rev. 12:11, NLT, emphasis added).

That last sentence describes the crucified life. If your past is completely nailed to Christ's cross, then there's no reason for shame or embarrassment. Your record of wrongs should no longer haunt you, and you should no longer fear the opinion of others.

When I arose from Satan's attack on my life, it was like bursting forth from a tomb. The guilt and shame that attempted to keep me in the grave could no longer hold me down. The past had lost its influence. Rather than shut me up, the whole experience only emboldened me to speak up. I arose that day determined to use my story to bring others back to the cross, and I didn't care what anyone thought.

Having said this, some are concerned about how much we should share about the things we've been through. I don't suggest you air out all of your dirty laundry. It's possible to expose so much detail that your former struggles become more exalted than your victory. And if we're not careful, people will use our pasts as a license for their sin. Remember, we are to boast in the victory of Christ that changed our lives, not glory in how bad we were before.

My point in all of this is that you shouldn't be afraid to share your story. Certainly be sensitive to the timing of the Holy Spirit, and speak only when He directs you. But don't be embarrassed by it.

If you still feel squeamish about sharing, begin with small opportunities. Bring up parts of your testimony in casual conversations with close friends. Base a social network post upon it. Write a short blog. Each time you share, another nail goes through the influence of your past until it's completely crucified to you. Then, larger opportunities will arise.

Sharing your story releases hope.

Each one of us was rescued and brought out of something (Col. 1:13). You and I were once drowning in guilt and shame, and the cross was our lifesaver. The cross remains the means by which we stay afloat. But there's a purpose behind all of this. God went to great lengths to chase after us, rescue us, and adopt us into His family for a reason.

> But you are a chosen race, a royal priesthood, a holy
> nation, God's own people, in order that you may

proclaim the mighty acts of him who called you out of darkness into his marvelous light.

—1 PETER 2:9

You and I were rescued from death in order that we will *proclaim* the mighty acts of God! We are to revel and boast in His power. Like Jesus, we are charged to show our scars to those around us and reveal, "Here stands someone who should be dead but is now alive."

In these dark days it's critical that people see the hope of resurrection. More than ever people need confidence that God is real, that He loves them, and that He can really transform their lives into something of value. Transformed people transform people! So as one who's experienced that transformation, your story has the power to release that hope.

Perhaps your story will encourage the addict that freedom can be had. The sick that their symptoms are not the final answer. The depressed that there is a place of exceeding joy. The outcast that there is acceptance. The worried that God will provide. No matter how big or small, your story might be just the hope that someone needs to make it through whatever he or she faces today. Don't hold it back.

Gotcha, Devil!

You've now come to the place that Satan has always feared. He knows that greater than anything else, your voice is a formidable force against his influence in the lives of so many others. He's afraid that your story will provide others with the evidence that what God did for you, He will also do for them. And so he gave it his best to shut you up. Long ago he set you up to fail and then aimed to convince you that you weren't good enough—that God can't use you. But he's the one who failed!

The cross dethroned him, the blood speaks against him, and

now your mind is fixed on victory! Stand today in the truth you know: *God created you; God loves you; God can and will use you.* God will use the story of your wounds to share the story of His. And through this many more will enter His family. What greater plan and purpose is there than this?

Don't let up, give up, back up, or shut up! It's time to speak up! Through the blood of the Lamb and the testimony of its transformation, you hold the power over your past and with it the ability to silence Satan and live victoriously. Indeed, the very things that Satan intended for your defeat have actually defeated him instead.

"Gotcha, devil!"

MORE SATAN-SILENCING SCRIPTURES TO SPEAK ALOUD

AS WE EXPLORED IN CHAPTER 11, THE WORD OF God is a weapon (Eph. 6:17). And speaking it aloud is how we use it offensively against the devil. I explained how I found that personalizing Scripture upon notecards was an effective way for me to silence Satan throughout the day.

Still, at times I became too lazy or tended to forget to do this. And as we know, a weapon is ineffective unless it's used. One day I inquired of the Lord for a better strategy to help me remember. "I need something that's always with me, something that I can't forget," I requested. Then I received a download straight from heaven. A smartphone app. "That's it!" I boasted. I determined that day to develop an app that puts the power of the Word of God in your pocket to silence Satan whenever and wherever he attacks.

A few months later, we released the Shut Up, Devil! app to the world. It contains categories so that you can quickly iden-tity common feelings such as fear, guilt, or temptation. Within each category are digital cards that you can swipe through. These each contain a relevant scripture and a personalized version designed so that you can easily speak it aloud. You can also favorite specific cards for quick access later.

The real power is in its reminder system, which alerts you as often or as little as you like. Setting these reminders is extremely useful to help you stay on the offensive and keep Satan silenced in your life.

Download the Shut Up, Devil! app free today at www.shutup devil.org.

For those of you who can't get access to the app or want some instant encouragement now, below is a short list of personalized Scriptures on common issues that you're bound to face.

Addiction

I will not let myself by overcome by evil, but I will overcome evil with good (Rom. 12:21).

Anger

I follow the example of the Lord, who is slow to anger and full of love. I have great mercy and love for those around me (Ps. 103:8).

Anxiety

I don't worry about anything. Instead I seek first the kingdom of God and His righteousness, and I trust that all of my needs will be met (Matt. 6:31–33).

Depression

I live refreshed and full of joy because God is my comfort and encouragement (2 Cor. 7:6).

Fear

God has not given me a spirit of fear or shyness. Instead I have power, love, and self-discipline (2 Tim. 1:7).

Finances

God will supply everything that I need according to His riches in glory by Christ Jesus (Phil. 4:19).

Guilt

I'm in Christ, and therefore I'm a new creation. My record of wrongs is erased, and I'm no longer defined by my past or mistakes, but I have a fresh new start! (2 Cor. 5:17).

Health

At the cross Jesus bore my sins on His body, so I'm free from sin and live in righteousness. Because of His wounds I have been healed (1 Pet. 2:24).

Loneliness

I have no wants other than a relationship with God, who says He will never leave me or forsake me (Heb. 13:5).

Lust

I clothe myself in Christ, and I stop thinking about indulging my flesh and its lustful desires (Rom. 13:14).

Rejection

God has chosen me to be a part of His family through Jesus Christ. In His family I'm loved and accepted (Eph. 1:5–6).

Stress

In my weariness I come to Jesus, and He gives me rest. I work with Him and learn from Him, for His yoke is easy and His burden is light. He refreshes my soul (Matt. 11:28–30).

Temptation

I submit myself to God. I resist the devil, and he must flee from me. I draw near to God, and He draws near to me (James 4:7–8).

Unloved

God loves me so much that He gave His only Son, so that I, who believe in Him, will not perish but will have eternal life (John 3:16).

NOTES

Chapter 1
You've Been Set Up

1. Glenn Croston, "The Thing We Fear More Than Death," *The Real Story of Risk* (blog), PsychologyToday.com, November 28, 2012, http://www.psychologytoday.com/blog/the-real-story-risk/201211/the-thing-we-fear-more-death (accessed April 8, 2014).

2. Thom S. Rainer and Jess Rainer, *The Millennials: Connecting to America's Largest Generation* (Nashville: B&H Books, 2011), 117.

3. *New Oxford American Dictionary*, 2nd ed., Erin McKean, ed. (New York: Oxford University Press, 2005), s.v. "setup."

4. Matthew Henry, *Matthew Henry's Commentary on the Whole Bible: Complete and Unabridged in One Volume* (Peabody, MA: Hendrickson, 1994), s.v. "John 10:1–18."

5. *New Oxford American Dictionary*, s.v. "advantage."

Chapter 2
The Profile of the Accuser

1. Holley Gerth, "No Matter What You've Done…God Is Not Done With You," *Holley Gerth* (blog), http://holleygerth.com/no-matter-what-youve-done-god-is-not-done-with-you/ (accessed April 8, 2014). Used by permission.

2. GemSelect.com, "Gemstone Information Center," http://www.gemselect.com/gem-info/gemstone-information-center.php (accessed April 8, 2014).

Chapter 3
The Devil's Playbook

1. For more information on this, watch my interview "Overcoming Wounds of the Past" with Barbara Stephens, http://www.kylewinkler

.org/videos/mama-hug-how-to-overcome-shame/ (accessed April 9, 2014).

2. Bob Sullivan, "ID Theft on the Rise Again: 12.6 Million Victims in 2012, Study Shows," NBCNews.com, February 20, 2013, http://www.nbcnews.com/business/consumer/id-theft-rise-again-12-6-million-victims-2012-study-f1C8448021 (accessed April 9, 2014).

Chapter 4
The Noose or the Nails

1. As referenced in Bryan V. Hewing, "Judas, Jesus Christ and the 30 Pieces of Silver," Big B Files (blog), March 21, 2008, http://bigbfiles.wordpress.com/2008/03/21/judas-jesus-christ-and-the-30-pieces-of-silver/ (accessed April 9, 2014).

2. A. W. Tozer, The Radical Cross (Camp Hills, PA: Wingspread, 2009), 3.

Chapter 5
Behold the Lamb

1. New Oxford American Dictionary, s.v. "behold."

2. Charles H. Spurgeon, "Behold the Lamb!", sermon preached July 14, 1872, Metropolitan Tabernacle, Newington, Spurgeon's Sermons, vol. 18 (1872), Christian Classics Ethereal Library, http://www.ccel.org/ccel/spurgeon/sermons18.xxxiii.html (accessed April 9, 2014).

3. Charles H. Spurgeon, "The Lamb of God in Scripture," sermon preached October 8, 1893, at Metropolitan Tabernacle, Newington, http://www.spurgeon.org/sermons/2329.htm (accessed April 9, 2014).

4. Martin Luther, On the Freedom of a Christian, viewed at Fordham University, Modern History Sourcebook, http://www.fordham.edu/halsall/mod/luther-freedomchristian.asp (accessed April 10, 2014).

Chapter 6
The Blood That Speaks

1. Bruce N. Fisk, "Unavoidable Gore, Controversy in 'Passion?'," ABCNews.com, February 14, http://abcnews.go.com/WNT/story?id=131509&page=1&singlePage=true (accessed April 10, 2014).

2. Ibid.

3. "Nothing but the Blood" by Robert Lowry. Public domain.

4. "There Is Power in the Blood" by Lewis F. Jones. Public domain.

5. Rob Bell, Love Wins (New York: Harper Collins, 2011), 128.

6. Teens Health From Nemours, "Blood," http://kidshealth.org/
teen/your_body/body_basics/blood.html (accessed April 10, 2014).

Chapter 7
Marching 'em Naked

1. Herschel H. Hobbs, *My Favorite Illustrations* (Nashville:
Broadman Press, 1990.)

2. S. Michael Houdmann, "What Is the Difference Between Iniquity, Sin, and Transgression?", GotQuestions.org, http://www
.gotquestions.org/iniquity-sin-transgression.html (accessed April 10,
2014).

Chapter 8
No Loitering!

1. *New Oxford American Dictionary*, s.v. "loiter."

2. Joanne Taylor, "Seeds for Success, Pt. 2: A Seed Must Die Before
It Grows," Examiner.com, April 13, 2010, http://www.examiner.com/
article/seeds-for-success-pt-2-a-seed-must-die-before-it-grows (accessed
April 10, 2014).

Chapter 9
The Place of God's Delight

1. Marc Lewis, "The Science of Craving," *Addicted Brains* (blog),
PsychologyToday.com, February 21, 2012, http://www
.psychologytoday.com/blog/addicted-brains/201202/the-science
-craving (accessed April 10, 2014).

2. Ibid.

Chapter 10
The Uniform of the Righteous

1. Amie Gordon, "The Power of a Police Uniform: An Instinct to
Obey Authority," *Psych Wednesdays* (blog), *Berkeley Science Review*, July
27, 2011, http://sciencereview.berkeley.edu/the-power-of-the-police
-uniform-an-instinct-to-obey-authority/ (accessed April 11, 2014).

2. Kids Health From Nemours, "Your Digestive System," http://
kidshealth.org/kid/htbw/digestive_system.html (accessed April 11,
2014).

Chapter 11
Shut Up, Devil!

1. United Bible Societies, "Bible Translation," http://www
.unitedbiblesocieties.org/sample-page/bible-translation/ (accessed April
11, 2014).

2. As quoted on GoodReads.com, "Martin Luther Quotes," http://
www.goodreads.com/quotes/109877-so-when-the-devil-throws-your
-sins-in-your-face (accessed April 11, 2014).

Chapter 12
The Voice of Truth

1. Gary Hardin, "Humility," in *Holman Illustrated Bible Dictionary,*
ed. Chad Brand et al. (Nashville: Holman Bible Publishers, 2003), 792.

Chapter 13
Speak Up!

1. Based on Carol Kornacki, *A Soul for Sale* (N.p.: A&A Books,
2010); see also my interview with Carol Kornacki, available at http://
www.kylewinkler.org/videos/carol-kornacki (accessed April 11, 2014).
Used by permission.

2. Merriam-Webster.com, s.v. "testimony," http://www.merriam
-webster.com/dictionary/testimony (accessed April 11, 2014).

ACKNOWLEDGMENTS

THROUGHOUT MY LIFE I'VE PRAYED FOR MENTORS. I crave learning from those who have forged the paths before me and often have the scars and stories to prove it. As I reflect upon my journey thus far, I clearly see that my prayer was answered. God has blessed me with so many positive influences and everyday heroes, many whose voices are represented deep within the thoughts and theology of this book.

First, I extend my greatest thanks to the three "Drs" who provided the utmost support and contributions to this project.

Dr. Leo Carney, my closest brother in the Lord, and an unwavering voice of encouragement, accountability, and reason: Day after day you patiently listened to me ramble as I fleshed out all of my challenges. You never once refused to proofread and edit nearly every one of my writings! Through it all you've remained my greatest supporter. I love encountering God with you. I'm forever changed because of the friendship I've found in you, your wife, and children.

Dr. Jim Harris, my coach and friend: The Lord sure knew what He was doing when He connected us at that Sunday school picnic through a discussion about the latest smartphone.

Since then you've become one of the greatest "impacters" in my life, both professionally and personally. You're a model of character, competence, courage, and commitment—one that I pray I grow to reflect. Thank you for your relentless exhortations.

Dr. Sandy Kirk, my fellow revolutionary: You brought me back to the cross! Your life's message is the single greatest influence upon this book. Thank you for tirelessly pouring into a generation that many people have dismissed. This book is just one of the countless fruits of your selfless labors.

To my editor, Jevon Bolden, and the team at Charisma Media—thank you for believing in this project and in me. You all are first class, and I appreciate your hard work to help bring this message to the masses.

So many others have significantly influenced my faith journey: Pastors Ron and Connie Coleman, Pastors Derek and Karen Doiron, Denise Moore, Denise Walsh, Larry Sparks, Pat Schatzline, and Pastor Buford Lipscomb. You all have been walking sermons in my life and have each spoken words into me that I will never forget.

Finally, to my mom and dad: Your strong commitment to faith laid the foundation upon which I now stand. You have a mighty legacy in the family you raised. Thank you for accepting God's plan for my life, even when it didn't always make sense. It's only just beginning. I love you.

ABOUT THE AUTHOR

KYLE WINKLER IS A LEADING VOICE FOR A GENERA-tion not satisfied with casual or powerless faith. He is the founder of Kyle Winkler Ministries, a media and teaching ministry through which tens of thousands have been impacted worldwide by its television and Internet broadcasts, resources, and live speaking engagements. In 2014 Kyle launched the widely acclaimed mobile app Shut Up, Devil!, which stockpiles hundreds of scriptures as an innovative tool to combat doubt, fear, and many other issues commonly faced today.

Kyle's deep desire is to see people radically transformed by God's presence and power. Individuals of all ages relate to his passionate, practical messages in which he speaks openly about his life and the frequent temptations by memories of past hurts and rejection. Kyle is known for boasting about how daily encounters with God through the Word and worship are paramount to living an overcomer's life.

Before launching his own ministry, Kyle served in various political organizations; at one of the nation's fifteen largest churches—Christ Fellowship in Palm Beach Gardens, Florida;

and as the vice president of an international apologetics ministry. Kyle holds a master of divinity in biblical studies from Regent University in Virginia Beach, Virginia.

Kyle makes his home near the sun-soaked, white-sand beaches of Pensacola, Florida.

Connect with Kyle:

Web: www.kylewinkler.org
Facebook: www.facebook.com/kylejwinkler
Twitter: www.twitter.com/kylewinkler
YouTube: www.youtube.com/kylejwinkler

Schedule Kyle to speak:

scheduling@kylewinkler.org